# Widows Wear Stilettos

# Widows Wear Stilettos

## A Practical and Emotional Guide for the Young Widow

By
Carole Brody Fleet with
Syd Harriet, Ph.D., Psy.D.

New Horizon Press
Far Hills, NJ

New Horizon Press
P.O. Box 669
Far Hills, NJ 07931

Carole Brody Fleet with Syd Harriet, Ph.D., Psy.D.
Widows Wear Stilettos:
A Practical and Emotional Guide for the Young Widow

Cover design: Wendy Bass
Interior design: Susan Sanderson

Library of Congress Control Number: 2008925056

ISBN 13: 978-0-88282-339-3
ISBN 10: 0-88282-339-6
New Horizon Press

Manufactured in the U.S.A.

2013   2012   2011   2010   2009   /   5   4   3   2   1

# Authors' Note

This book is not intended to treat physical or emotional illness. All matters regarding personal health require medical supervision. A professional psychotherapist, counselor or other professional should be contacted in the case of prolonged symptoms and inability to function. Consultation with a medical doctor, a physical therapist and a nutritionist before committing to any exercises and recipes implemented in this publication is recommended.

For purposes of simplifying usage, the pronouns his or her and he or she are sometimes used interchangeably. The information, ideas, and suggestions contained in this book are not intended to replace any necessary therapy with mental health professionals.

All suggestions regarding medical, financial and legal subject matter are based upon the information, belief and personal opinions of Carole Brody Fleet with Syd Harriet, Ph.D., Psy.D. only and should not be construed as directed advice.

The strategies, exercises, diets and procedures in this book should be discussed with professionals in the appropriate fields.

Any application of the recommendations set forth in this book is at the reader's discretion and sole risk.

## DEDICATION

This book is lovingly dedicated to:

All widows everywhere; may your healing journeys be enhanced and enriched
and may your hearts and spirits be lifted and made stronger by the words in
this book.

The "Team"
My amazing mother, Eilene,
who gave me life;
and my beautiful daughter,
Kendall Leah,
who completed my life.
Without both of you, I could never be me
and I love you more than words will ever truly convey.

My father, Elvin "Clink" Clinkenbeard, of blessed memory.
February 2, 1923 – May 23, 2001
Daddy, thank you for blessing me with the joking sparkle in your eyes
and the warmth in your heart.
I am indeed now and will always be
"Daddy's Little Girl".

And to the late,
the great,
the inimitable
Michael Alan Fleet, Sr.,
of blessed memory.
July 21, 1945 – December 19, 2000
For your unconditional love
and for teaching me the true definition of courage.
Your legacy lives.
"Always and Forever Riding High"
With my undying love.

# TABLE OF CONTENTS

# INTRODUCTION

December 21, 2000. The sun was setting on a stereotypically beautiful California afternoon. Dozens of police officers stood at rapt attention; some with tears streaming down their faces, belying their attempts at stoicism. The soft moan of bagpipes echoed the traditional "Amazing Grace" over the hillsides. Several hundred more people stood staring at the flag-draped coffin with identically numb expressions—complete and utter disbelief. In one of my few moments of lucidity that day, watching this moment unfold as if it were happening to someone else and while holding tightly to our then-eleven-year-old daughter's hand, one lone thought continued to play over and over in my head:

*I'm a widow.*

Widowed. In my mind, widows are older, retired, with grown children and grandchildren. Widows are married for years and years and enjoy rich, full and storied lives with their spouses. Widows sport gray hair, live in retirement communities and go on a lot of cruises. Widows wear sensible shoes and entertain with stories of the "good old days" (penny candy, dime movies and Uncle Miltie) or the "bad old days" (the

Depression and, to paraphrase Bill Cosby's classic skit about his father, "Walking to school uphill both ways in ten feet of snow").

Conversely, I'm the last of the Baby Boomer generation. I came of age during Vietnam, Women's Rights and Watergate, pet rocks and puka shells, Led Zeppelin and lava lamps. My generation is "post-Pill and pre-AIDS"; ours is the generation that witnessed the birth of the microwave oven, the personal computer and the VCR and that remembers a life without MTV, cell phones, the Internet or reality television (well, unless you count *The Dating Game*).

Widowed? Impossible. I wear low-rise pants and miniskirts. Stiletto heels are the mainstay of my always-expanding wardrobe and, in fact, even the license plates on my car pay homage to my almost-fanatical love of all things footwear. I know all of the words to the *Rocky Horror Picture Show*—and not just the songs. My CD collection is heavily laden with 1970s disco and heavy metal and 1980s new wave, pop-punk and "hair band" music. Shopping is my zen. I'd rather dance than breathe. I love laughing till it hurts at comedy clubs and taking frequent trips to Las Vegas. I enjoy lemon drop martinis at sunset and a champagne cocktail with dinner (OK, I know the latter is a 1950s-era drink, but still...). My daughter and I share clothes and cheeseburgers, "girly time" and giggles.

*Yet I'm a widow.*

Widowed. An impossible concept; an even more preposterous reality to embrace. Still, at only forty years old, I was widowed—with a child to raise, mortgages to pay, the same "pile of bills" that every family in America has sitting on their respective desks, while in the midst of a veritable tornado of emotions and absolutely no idea how to transition into this new and unexpected life.

I attempted to seek support from others in my not-so-common position; those who were widowed at young ages with children to raise and sizeable chunks of life still in front of them—and found none. All of the widow/widower organizations, while certainly worthwhile, boasted membership consisting primarily of people in the somewhat older, here-are-pictures-of-my-grandchildren age group.

The Internet? The groups that I found were either determined to discuss nothing but their dearly departed and ONLY their dearly departed (which is fine for a little while, but certainly inhibits one's moving forward with life) or they were looking for dates, hardly what I needed at that season in my life.

Books? There are a lot of books out there; wonderful books on widowhood, grieving, loss, coping, coping with loss, coping with grieving, coping with widowhood, but none that I found dealt with <u>both</u> the practical issues of widowhood (whom to contact and how, what paperwork you'll need and helpful resources) and the many emotional issues that are particular to young widows.

In this book, I deal with many of the problems facing widows; therefore, much of what is written applies to widows of all ages. However, I have sought to explore issues that are specific to young widows, such as helping young and adolescent children transition and function in a world where "everyone has a dad except me"; re-entering the world of dating at a time when the large majority of your friends are married with families of their own; functioning as a "single" in a "couples" world without feeling like the cruise director on Noah's Ark; becoming sexually active again (or not); remarrying (or not); and so many other issues that affect women who are widowed at young ages.

Though you may feel all alone as a young widow, it is an unfortunate fact that the population of young widows has grown suddenly and dramatically—there are literally millions of us. It is indeed for those women to whom the title of widow has come far too soon that this book is intended. It is for those women to whom "till death do us part" happened long before it was ever expected; whether by long-term illness, sudden illness, accident or tragic circumstance.

Although your personal spirituality will be an integral part of your recovery, this book is a practical and emotional "road map" to help gently guide you through those first few challenging weeks and months as you phase into a new chapter of your life.

Throughout the book, there are "Cry and Carry On" alerts, referring to times during your personal healing journey when certain moments or events will trigger feelings of sometimes-overwhelming sadness. This is not to make you sad; rather, it's to let you know that not only is it normal, but also it's *perfectly all right to be sad* and then continue to move forward. There will also be sections labeled "From the Stiletto File": facts that I learned from personal experience, trial, a few errors and extensive research that I hope will help to ease your way through the practical changes that you must make as well as the emotional changes that you will undergo.

You'll also find areas for journaling, answering questions and exploring your own feelings and experiences in-depth so that you will actually be able to see your healing journey unfold in front of you. And, of course, there will be many tips and ideas—everything from suggestions on how to cope with the people around you; to recipes and quick exercise routines; to checklists so you can organize; to affirmations designed to uplift you as you progress on your healing journey.

I also want to strongly advise at the outset that if a significant period of time has passed (at least one year since the death) and you are finding that you have been unable to move forward; if you have difficulties eating, sleeping, functioning at work or with your children; if you are dependent upon alcohol or drugs (that are not expressly *prescribed* and *supervised* by a physician); or if you are engaging in any potentially destructive behaviors in order to deal with this painful experience, please immediately seek professional attention—there are wonderful, caring health professionals who are trained to deal with this very specialized area of grief.

Please let me reassure you that though you may feel like it right now, you are **not** alone. Let me also reassure you that even if you can't see it right now, today, at this moment, there is a big, beautiful life out there and together we will help you go get it.

### Chapter 1

# THERE'S A LIGHT
# AT THE END OF THE TUNNEL
## (And Trust Me, It's Not an Oncoming Train)

How do you even begin to describe the first few days and weeks after the death of your husband?

It's rather like trying to drive through the thickest, most impossibly dense fog; the kind where you can't even see the hood of your car. You're blind to what's in front of you, you have no idea what may be coming at you and it's just plain scary being out there all alone.

Where *do* you begin?

Where does the healing journey begin? How do you embark on your healing journey? How do you start to move forward, when in your mind, the world has just come crashing down around your ears?

These are most likely the very questions that are going through your mind right now, just as these were the very first questions that went through my mind the day after my husband's funeral. Since my husband was very ill, I knew that horrible moment in my life was imminent; yet one never truly expects the moment to actually arrive.

After an illustrious and highly-decorated career with the Santa Ana, California Police Department, my husband, Michael Fleet Sr., retired on

September 14, 1998, only to be diagnosed at the age of fifty-three with amyotrophic lateral sclerosis (ALS or what is more commonly known as Lou Gehrig's Disease) two weeks after his retirement. With that diagnosis came the cruel reality that at some point in the not-too-distant future, our daughter Kendall and I were going to be alone. Mike battled his illness bravely and faced his future with courage, dignity and humor. However, on December 19, 2000, the end came peacefully, at home, as was Mike's wish.

Mike's was an extremely large funeral; the funeral director had said that it was the second-largest funeral that they ever handled. Officers from police departments throughout California and the southwestern United States were there, as well as officials from all manner of government agencies. It was a day rich in remembrance, tradition and honor for a man who deserved it all and then some.

Then the next morning came…and we were all alone. Everyone had gone home and "gone on"; that was certainly to be expected. But the "what now" echoed through my mind, over and over—not knowing what to do, where to start or even having ambition enough to get out of my flannel penguin-print pajamas with the feet on them.

So I didn't.

Not the very next day anyway. Not even the day after that. I'm fairly certain that I didn't even get off the couch.

This book deals with a very serious subject by using a little bit of humor peppered throughout—humor has always been my favorite outlet. Despite the subject matter and in spite of how badly you may be feeling right now, I'm sure that you will see at least one thing in this book to which you will both directly relate and laugh—maybe even out loud! However, to get to the laughter, you do go through the seemingly endless period of tears. As much as we would all love to skip over the crying and go straight to the laughter, your emotional recovery must start at the very beginning.

So where do you begin?

Immediately after and/or since your husband's death, how many of the following feelings have you experienced? How many of these feelings are still a regular part of your life? And be honest with yourself, it's just us here:

Fear

Loneliness

Despair

Overwhelming sadness

Anger

Anxiety

Irritability

Confusion

Disbelief/Denial

Lack of ambition

Lack of or inability to sleep

Loss of appetite or emotional overeating

Lack of interest in normal daily activities

Loss of purpose

Feelings of abandonment

Feelings of worthlessness

Feeling as if life is no longer worth living

How many did you choose? Two? Seven? All of them? If you selected every single one of these feelings, you will be pleased to know that you are absolutely, without a doubt, 100 *percent normal*! However, while all of these feelings may be evident, the one feeling that we must address in all seriousness and without delay, is feeling as though life is without purpose or is no longer worth living without your husband.

If your husband experienced a long-term illness prior to his death (as did mine), you likely dedicated every waking moment (and most of the otherwise-sleeping moments) to his care. His illness governed every decision, every action and every single plan you made each day. Now that your husband—and the illness—is no longer with you, you wake up in the morning and, in addition to the tragic loss of your husband, you don't know what to do with yourself and all of this "extra" time stretching out in front of you. In other words, your whole "purpose" for getting out of bed every day—is gone.

If your husband died suddenly, the solid foundation on which you were standing only yesterday has just opened up like an earthquake fault line and has swallowed you whole and without any warning. Whether your loss was due to accident, sudden illness or tragic circumstance, all you know is that one morning your husband was here and that evening you were all alone, reeling from shock, numb with grief and not having the first idea in which direction you should turn.

However his death occurred, your husband is gone and let's face it, he isn't supposed to be gone. He is supposed to be here to play Santa Claus to the kids, fix the broken rain gutters, pick up the pizza on the way home from work, send you flowers on Valentine's Day, teach your children how to drive, take the pictures before the senior prom and dance with you on New Year's Eve. He's supposed to be here to laugh with you, cry with you, celebrate with you, fight like hell with you, make up with you, plan retirement with you, vacation with you. In your heart and mind you feel like this is absolute insanity; women are NOT widowed at your age. Yet he's not here anymore, so what's the point of even going on?

In fact, your feelings are normal and even true, but difficult to cope with.  Sorry, I'm not letting you off the hook that easily.

Here's where I suppose I should grab my pom-poms and tell you how you have to go on for "the children's sake" (which is a good reason, but isn't reason enough in and of itself) or I could spout platitudes about how wonderful life is and break into a chorus about the sun coming out tomorrow and all. However, if you're a brand new young widow, you just can't see that yet. You might not see that sun coming out even after time has passed. So one step at a time, let's gently examine some of the very first steps to take during this early period of grief.

## Books/Audiovisual Aids

The very fact that you are reading this book is a positive and vital first step in the right direction. Not only are you beginning or continuing your journey and your healing process, but also you are truly interested in and dedicated to healing yourself and your children. I applaud you for taking this very first step. However, the important thing is for you to continue on your way—don't stop with this book!

In my former career as a sales director with a major cosmetics company, one of my favorite job responsibilities was the training, mentoring and teaching of beauty consultants. As much as I loved this aspect of my job, however, I also seized every opportunity to have these consultants listen to and learn from many other experts within the company. I found that as teachers and mentors, not only do we all have different viewpoints and opinions, but also the consultants often discovered new and exciting ideas for growing successful businesses.

The same philosophy applies here. There are many superb books concerning grief and loss and I highly recommend that you read at least two or three additional books on the subject. Surround yourself with knowledge and comfort; allow it to envelop you. If you don't have the time to sit and read a whole bunch of books (and let's face it, many of us don't), get books on audio or spoken-word self-help CDs. Although this book is written by someone who is sitting in the young widows' "front seat" right along with you, I believe that it is quite healthy to get several different perspectives on the subject.

## Don't Do This Alone

When it comes to challenge, stress or turmoil, let me share an illustration that I always use as a teaching tool. Take a can of soda and start shaking it up and down vigorously. On the outside, the can looks fine, but on the inside, there's a storm brewing—and just because you can't see that storm brewing inside the can does not mean that it isn't happening. Guess what's going to happen eventually? At some point, that can is going to explode into one big mess. Think of yourself as that soda can. Even though by all outward appearances you may be doing "just fine", and no doubt you are telling people that, you have been shaken up and down. Without releasing what's going on inside of you at some point, an explosion is going to occur—it's inevitable.

I'm sure that you've heard the following saying over and over when you've been watching television commercials, "Don't try this at home". For our purposes, I'm changing that saying to "Don't *do* this alone". Although dealing with people is probably the very last thing that you're up for right now, talking about and releasing what's going on inside of you is essential. Even if you don't consider yourself a "talker", even if you believe that you can "manage" all by yourself, PLEASE talk to someone. Let's avoid that "soda can" explosion.

To whom should you turn? Although family members and friends are loving, concerned and well-meaning, though they are not "the widow", they too have experienced the loss of your husband within their different perspectives and therefore may not be in the best possible position to help you heal. Additionally, though some family and friends feel all too free to tell you what they think you "should" be doing and how they think you "should" be handling things, this isn't necessarily helpful or therapeutic.

The choice would be to seek out and turn to:

1.  A member of the clergy if you are affiliated with a house of worship. Even if you are not necessarily a deeply spiritual person, many clerics are well-trained in the areas of grief, loss and crisis intervention.

2.  Your family or primary physician. You can either confide in him/her directly or request a referral.

3.  An expert in the mental health profession—a psychiatrist, psychologist or family therapist.

4.  Hospice directors or liaisons, social workers and funeral directors, who all have extensive experience in this area. In fact, many hospice programs and mortuary counselors will "stay" with you to provide counsel for the entire first year following your husband's death. Avail yourself of their compassion, advice and expertise.

Some feel most comfortable speaking with a person who knows them, their family and their situation well. There are also those who may feel more comfortable talking with someone who doesn't know them quite as well; perhaps they need a little more objectivity or "distance". Whatever the case, you need not and you should not go through this early phase of grief by yourself.

Lastly, don't forget to seek out support from others who have been and/or are currently in similar situations to your own! Just knowing that you are not all by yourself on your healing journey through grief will afford you more comfort than you'll ever realize. You'll meet thousands of women very much like you at **www.widowswearstilettos.com** and, I believe, you will discover that you do not have to be alone on your own journey.

## One Moment of Despair is Just That...ONE MOMENT

It's quite likely that you have never felt this alone and that you feel like no one really understands what it is you're going through. Rest assured, I get it. So does every other young widow out there, and there are a lot of us, believe me. You may be in a place right now where there seems to be only "one way out"—when the pain is so bad that it's a physical ache and you truly can't see a solution or even how you will get through the next days. The loneliness is overwhelming; the nights are endless and you can almost taste the sadness.

If you are feeling desperate as if you don't want to live any longer, I am imploring you to **GET HELP IMMEDIATELY**. Please skip right now to the end of this book for a list of resources that will help you in this moment of crisis. I promise you that whatever the feelings of despair, helplessness, loneliness and pain you are feeling right now, there IS help, there IS remedy and there IS a tomorrow. **You** have the choice NOT to permit your husband's death to claim more than one life. Whatever the circumstances surrounding your husband's death, those circumstances have taken one life already—decide that those circumstances do NOT merit two lives. Get stubborn, get ornery and get absolutely determined. Don't give in and *please don't give up*! You do not yet realize the depth of your strength and though you may not feel like it at this moment, you will soon learn that you are stronger than you even realize. Take heart, take hold, take a loving and helping hand—we are going to get you through this!

## JUST FOR YOU

Always remember—the difference between hope and despair can be as simple as a filling meal, a good night's sleep and knowing that at least one person out there understands.

## WIDOWS WEAR STILETTOS "HEART MONITOR"

One of the most positive first steps that you can take on your healing journey is identifying the feelings to which you relate the strongest. One of the best ways to actually *see* your healing journey in progress is to *write* about it—and no, not on a computer "blog"! Let's find out how you're feeling right now. Grab a pen:

- Return to the list of feelings earlier in this chapter. Understanding that you have likely experienced all of these feelings at some point, select the *five* predominant feelings that affect you the most or that you believe you're dealing with on a daily or regular basis.

_____

_____

_____

_____

_____

- What are the most common "trigger mechanisms" for your feelings; for example, a certain time of day, a place that you have to pass on your way to work, attending church or synagogue, etc?

_____

_____

_____

_____

_____

- After reading this chapter, how are you feeling right now, at this very minute?

_____

_____

- What is the one thing that you feel may be holding you back from progressing forward on your healing journey?

_____

_____

_____

- List three things that you either have done or that you want to do to help overcome whatever it is that you feel is preventing you from moving forward.

_____

_____

_____

_____

_____

- Select one person (who is not a family member) in whom you can comfortably confide and share your feelings. Choose someone to whom you can turn if and when you need to speak with someone. If you don't know this person right now, to whom would you feel the most comfortable being referred? (A therapist, a physician, a cleric, etc.)

_____

- If you feel the need to be referred to a professional, write down the name of a person who will provide you with that referral, along with his or her telephone number and on what day you are going to "calendar" the call for that referral.

_____

Just by taking the time to answer these questions and set forth a plan of action, you have already begun to take control of your grief, put your feelings into a healthy perspective and most importantly, you have officially begun—or are moving forward on—your healing journey! Congratulations and let's move forward together!

### Chapter 2

# PEOPLE SAY THE DUMBEST THINGS

### (Or: "You Did Not Just Say That!")

I feel obligated to inform you that unfortunately, throughout your healing process, you are going to hear comments from people that are just plain DUMB; at least that's been my experience. What's more, I know that you are right this second nodding in agreement—that, or you're laughing out loud, perhaps even both!

Long ago, legendary radio and television host Art Linkletter starred in a radio and television show entitled *Kids Say the Darndest Things*. These were wonderfully endearing shows, during which he asked young children questions about all sorts of things. The children responded with incredible guilelessness and sometimes hysterically funny observations on everything from school rules to how Mommy and Daddy get along (or not!) at home. The equally-talented Bill Cosby hosted a television show in recent years by the same name based upon the same concept: that children *do* say the darndest things. Why? Because they're children and in most cases have no discernable diplomacy skills, no edit buttons and they process what they observe in the simplest form—brute honesty—relating observations in the best way that they know how.

However, adults are supposed to "know better". Adults are supposed to know things and exercise good judgment like, "If you can't say something nice, say nothing at all." Or at the very least, "Say it to yourself silently first before you say it out loud and subsequently say the wrong thing or worse, say something very hurtful." Please allow me to share some of my particular favorite "consolations", as well as the "responses" that went through my mind upon hearing these "pearls", if only just to let you know that you are not alone in what you're being told right now:

- **"At least you were prepared"** or, **"It's not like it wasn't expected"** or, **"At least you had time together to prepare (you'll generally hear this if your spouse has died after a long illness).**

    Since my husband Mike's illness lasted over two years, I heard this "pearl" more than any other—as if having "time to prepare" made the eventuality less painful. As if knowing to expect death made the reality any easier.

    Newsflash to anyone who may have ever uttered these words: It *doesn't*.

    You see, even though we knew that Mike's was a terminal illness, the feeling of impending doom was still only a concept. It is true that because we knew he was going to die, I was able to discuss practical matters with Mike ahead of time and make arrangements according to Mike's specific wishes about two months prior to his death. We also had the opportunity to talk a lot about what the future held. Did it make the **reality** of his death any less difficult to bear? Not even a little bit. There is absolutely no such thing as "being prepared" for the loss of your husband.

- **"At least he didn't suffer." (You'll hear this if your spouse dies after a short illness, accident or tragedy.)**

    That made things easier on him…not you.

- **"It was his time."**

    His time? What time exactly is that? I don't own that wristwatch, do you?

- **"It's God's will"** or, **"Everything happens for a reason."**

    I am a deeply spiritual person. I do believe that there is a God and that everything happens for a reason, according to His plan. I have also derived great comfort through my particular set of beliefs. However, I didn't find any comfort in hearing about God's will; especially when I couldn't begin to imagine what "reason" God would have for "taking" my husband away from me and from his family. You probably won't find any comfort in such statements either. Regardless of religious denomination or conviction, I don't imagine God or any higher power "willing" suffering or pain of any kind to anyone.

- **"God never gives you more than you can handle."**

     Don't you wish that sometimes God didn't have quite so much confidence in what we are able to handle?

- **"You were just meant to be alone."**

     If that were the case, you would be a hermit, living in a cave someplace. If I were meant to be alone or sought to be alone, I certainly would not have gotten married and I'm pretty confident that I would not have reproduced. I was NOT meant to be alone. Since you too are a widow, this means you obviously did not choose to be alone. You met, fell in love with and built a life with another person. No one, but NO ONE—on earth or elsewhere—"meant" for you to be alone.

- **"I know how you feel"** or, **"I understand what you're going through." (This statement is generally followed by his or her own particular "tale of woe", during which you suddenly will become the one doing the consoling rather than the bereaved needing consolation.)**

     Allow me to share an absolutely charming story. Immediately following Mike's death, the students in my daughter Kendall's sixth grade class each made sympathy cards for her—these handmade, homespun cards were immensely comforting to us both. One card in particular made me laugh out loud. It was from a girl who, after expressing her sympathy at Mike's death, went on to state, "I know how you feel—my rat died."

     This is a perfect example of what I stated earlier: that children relate the best way that they know how and the loss of this child's dear departed rat was the only way that this precious little girl knew to relate to Kendall's pain. I hasten to add, however, that adult responses should be different. Consequently, unless one has traveled your particular road, no one has any idea how you feel or what you're going through. None.

- **"You're too young to be a widow."**

No kidding. Like this was some kind of career choice. But then again, he's too young to be gone. Enough said.

- **"You're young and pretty. You'll find someone else."**

The fact that we are young and/or pretty is irrelevant. It is of absolutely no consolation and it certainly does not make us feel any better to hear this just after having buried our husbands. I can further assure you that there isn't a widow among us who went on a manhunt for "someone else" right after the funeral—and sadly, that is when most widows hear this statement!

- **"This will make you stronger."**

If this is what it takes to become stronger, I prefer a great big heaping helping of weakness, thank you.

- **"Life goes on."**

I'm still trying to think of a response that sounds more intelligent than, "Well, DUH!!" I have yet to come up with one.

- **"Now you'll have closure."**

Another newsflash: There is *no such thing* as "closure" when your spouse has died and I, for one, wish that we could blast this word out of the dictionary and off of the planet. Closure, I feel, is something that surgeons do when they're finished with operations. Closure is what happens to the fast lane on the freeway after a fender-bender has taken place, inevitably during rush hour. We will further explore the myth that is "closure" in chapter 12 entitled, "Now You'll Have Closure (And Other Myths Laid to Rest)".

- **"You'll forget all about him when you get a new boyfriend."**

This "pearl" was my personal favorite and, years later, I am still astonished that someone actually said this to me in total earnest and seriousness – and *at the funeral!* Someone actually believed that a "new boyfriend" would somehow replace the dashed future, the broken plans, the shattered hopes and the dreams that Mike and I had as a couple and as a family. That another man would make me "forget" about the one person whom I loved and who loved me above anyone else. That all I needed to do was to simply "slot" someone into the space that Mike had left and my "former life" would fade away—as if I would want it to! I cannot come up with an adequate adjective to describe exactly how I felt when this person made this statement. I do recall that I was momentarily overcome with a very strong desire to drive staples into her forehead.

So, how do you respond to these foolish statements, especially when some of them are, at best, downright absurd; at worst, a seemingly total insult and given at a traumatic time when you are likely low on patience, nutrition, sleep and edit buttons of your own?

Nod and smile.

I know. You don't like that answer and frankly, I didn't care for it much myself. However, this is what you must remember—somewhere in the fogbank that has taken the place of rational thought immediately after death:

## No one means any genuine harm

No matter how hurtful and harmful these statements seem (and they do), at the heart of every single one of these statements is sincere and legitimate concern. The reality is that most people simply don't know what to say or how to react when the news of death arrives. For example, someone who tells you that "you're too young to be a widow" has the same mental picture of widows that I described earlier. You obviously don't fall into that widow "category"; therefore, it logically follows that you must be too young to actually *be* a widow. When you're told that you are "young and pretty", it is likely meant not only as a compliment, but as a beacon of hope as well—a sincere effort to point out that you will once again be able to find love and companionship in your life.

Someone who says, "I know what you're going through", though perhaps not a widow, has no doubt experienced some kind of loss at some point in her life and is recalling her own grief in the hopes that you will not feel so alone. Even though it may feel like "one-upsmanship" to you and you're likely not in the mood to listen to someone else's stories of misery, he or she is truly making a sincere attempt to relate to your pain. Comments like "he didn't suffer" or "it was his time" are actually sincere attempts to bring you warmth and solace, as none of us wants to think that our beloved suffered in any way for even a second.

The "getting a new boyfriend" comment? I've got absolutely no explanation for that one.

Following is a "pledge" that you should read, reread and then cut out and keep in a place where you will see it often:

---

### CAROLE'S "I CANNOT BELIEVE WHAT PEOPLE ARE SAYING TO ME" PLEDGE

I understand that while people may say things to me that seem insensitive, idiotic or otherwise hurtful,
no one is intentionally trying to cause me further hurt or pain.
I realize that most people simply do not know what to say to me right now and that they are likely feeling uncomfortable under these circumstances.
Even though it may hurt me initially,
I will strive to take any such comments with a grain of salt.
Rather than getting hurt, irritated, wounded or offended,
I will instead nod and smile at the person or people who have made these comments, recognizing that the day will come when I will be able to laugh hysterically (or at least smile and shrug) at the comments and observations that I have endured.

You see, it's true that there will be times in widowhood that you will have to call upon all of your patience reserves and diplomacy skills of your own. You will have to remind yourself of the "nod and smile" at least one gazillion times and yes, in a weak moment, you will wonder and marvel at the stupidity of some people and the fact that they are permitted to operate motor vehicles. Nevertheless, nobody is intentionally "conspiring" to hurt your feelings—people really *are* looking for words of comfort and condolence to offer to you.

Shortly after Mike's death, I received a telephone call from a wonderful business colleague of mine. When news of Mike's death had reached her, she called me and said, "Carole, I'm so sorry. I cannot imagine the pain you are in right now." I took more comfort in those words than in anything anyone else could have said to me—because while she realized that she could not directly relate to what I was going through, she felt genuinely sorry for me and, in every sense of the definition of the word, sympathetic. I only wish that everyone had this brilliant woman's sensitivity, compassion and good old common sense; alas, that is not the case.

## JUST FOR YOU

This is truly where you will have to get hold of yourself and take it upon yourself to put others at ease. Don't let these seemingly insensitive comments ruin your day—or worse, ruin the relationship that you have with the person trying to convey sympathy. Instead, thank the person for his or her concern and let the individual know that you are doing "as well as can be expected" or words to that effect. One day soon, you too will laugh out loud at some of the things that people have said to you—and in turn, you will be so much wiser when you are in the important position of having to console another.

### WIDOWS WEAR STILETTOS "HEART MONITOR"

Let's have a little bit of fun and a giggle or two while we help you move past some of the hurt feelings that you may have recently experienced on your journey.

- Write down what you believe to be the five most irritating, insensitive, ridiculous or downright DUMB things that have been said to you since you became widowed. These might include some of the comments that you read in this chapter—that's fine. And, P.S., it's okay to laugh while you're doing this!

_____

_____

_____

_____

_____

- Upon hearing these comments, how did you initially feel? Hurt? Devastated? Furious? Or did you have to try to keep from laughing? Be honest!

_____

_____

_____

_____

_____

- Do you feel differently now? If so, how?

_____

_____

_____

_____

_____

## WIDOWS WEAR STILETTOS LAUGH-O-METER

Tell the truth: while you were reading this chapter and/or answering these questions, you giggled—or at least smiled once or twice didn't you? That's not only good news, but also it's *another* positive advance forward. Making these small changes are the way for us to continue on the healing journey—one positive move at a time. So feel free to smile, let's take the next step forward and be grateful that you're not the poor woman who, after her husband had passed away, was told by a none-too-diplomatic friend attending the funeral that she should get a dog to take her late husband's place.

### Chapter 3

# THINKING "INSIDE THE BOX"

## (For a Change)

Here you are, the weight of widowhood heavy on your shoulders; perhaps only for a short time; maybe for a long while now. This grief permeates every aspect of your life and, let's face it, every aspect of your life is just about "going through the motions" and "getting through" the day. It feels like you have to remind yourself to inhale and exhale; everything is a huge, almost tremendous effort. Smiling isn't genuine; walking feels like you're slogging through mud, just getting yourself out of bed feels overwhelming.

How on earth are you going to be able to "put your grief aside" in order to return to the office, prepare the meals, help with homework, chaperone the field trip, pay the bills and in general begin the arduous task of resuming life—because the resumption of life *feels* like the most grueling task you will ever undertake.

The ability to "compartmentalize" your life—to focus on one thing at a time, one activity at a time, one person at a time—is indeed a challenge. In this day and age where we all brag about and pride ourselves on multitasking, the art of compartmentalizing is virtually extinct. Just the proliferation of cell phones in our purses, cordless phones in our homes and computers that travel with us speak to our constant need to be doing more than one thing at a time—all of the time!

Admit it, you cook dinner while helping your child with spelling homework and signing permission slips for the field trip the next day; you're making grocery lists and doctor appointments while preparing an important presentation at work; you have driven on the freeway while eating a cheeseburger and French fries at the same time (Okay, I confess...that last example was about me).

Most of us do not have the luxury of spending all of our waking hours paying singular attention to our emotions at whim and at will. For example, approximately 80 percent of all women in the United States are employed in the workplace in one form or another; be it spare-time, part-time or full-time. The dismal fact is that the majority of corporate America allows a whopping *three days of leave* for bereavement for an immediate family member. Even if you use all of your accrued vacation and/or sick time on top of only three days off, that leaves very little time to plan and hold a funeral, initiate and follow up on all the many tasks and duties of the first days of widowhood. (We'll discuss these necessities in chapter 6, "The 'Business' of Widowhood".) In addition to all this, you need to begin your healing journey? The time slot is maybe two weeks total and that's if you're lucky and you have the time "saved".

At the time of Mike's death, I was self-employed. While being self-employed admittedly does have many wonderful advantages, not the least of which is the distinct benefit of being able to set your own hours, it also means two other very important things:

1. You do not "get to work whenever you want." Realistically, you often are working when you would really rather not. Discipline and a work ethic are essential, since this ultimately determines whether or not your business is successful.

2. If you don't go to work, you aren't making any money. Banks and creditors tend to be critical when you're not paying debts. There's no such thing as paid sick leave or paid bereavement leave when you're self-employed: you "show up" or the bills don't get paid. Pure and simple.

If you're a stay-at-home mom, the pressure is no less. In many respects, your job is even more difficult than returning to a job outside of the home, for the simple reason that there really is no such thing as "time off". Schoolwork continues, children's activities continue, clothes get dirty, floors need washing, teeth need fixing, colds get caught. The laundry list is endless and you don't get to "call in sick" or "call in tired" or "call in" period.

So, how do you cope? *When* do you cope? How do you return to your life *and* grieve at the same time?

As women of the twenty-first century, we have all been taught to strive to "live a balanced life". Pick up any women's magazine or the myriad number of books on the subject and what are we told? We're told that we can and should "have it all". Further, if we don't "have it all", if our lives aren't in "perfect balance" with "X" amount of set hours in a day for career, family, emotional self and spiritual self, it's our own fault, we are failing ourselves or our children or we're living a life "out of balance".

Despite true economic necessity for being there in the first place, women in the workplace have been made to feel guilty for "neglecting their families". The stay-at-home mother has been made to feel like a left-behind-throwback to an era gone by. It's all enough to make your head spin! If all this wasn't enough, now you've had this devastation in your life and whatever balance you once had has been completely thrown off.

We, as widows and as women, need to STOP IT RIGHT NOW!

At the risk of being controversial (which has never really bothered me), I'm going to go ahead and declare that, along with the fact that the emperor is not wearing any clothes and that no-carb diets are stupid, it is also impossible to have a "perfect balance" of life under the best of circumstances, let alone under the circumstances with which you are dealing right now.

As we deal with grief, we must learn to compartmentalize our lives in the best way that we know how. For example, I am a mother, I am a writer, I am a woman with strong religious faith and—SURPRISE—I'm also a "girl". Am I giving 100 percent of me to all of these roles at the same time, every single day? Absolutely not. When I'm writing, it doesn't mean that I'm no longer a spiritual person; it just means that at that moment, my emphasis is not on the spiritual. When I'm out with my girlfriends, does it mean that I'm not a mother or that I don't care about my child? Of course not. It simply means that for those few hours, my focus is not on parenting (although I do admit that my cell phone does stay on—just in case).

No one is 100 percent of all of their roles all of the time. However, whatever it is that you are doing in a given moment, you need to be fully "there" in that activity, be it time spent with your children, time spent at the office or on the tennis court. This is called "compartmentalizing" and it is what you will also learn in this book to do with your grief. By learning to compartmentalize, you will be able to return to the productive day-to-day activities that comprise your life *as well as* have time for you, your grief and your healing journey. In other words, we are going to "think *inside* the box" and that box has a whole bunch of different sections—just like your makeup case.

Learning the art of compartmentalizing is a discipline; it doesn't simply happen overnight. This is especially the case when you are dealing with this kind of grief—the kind of grief that can sneak up and "bite" you when you least expect it, even after time has passed and the pain has lessened with time. You know what I mean: you hear that certain song, you smell his cologne when passing the department store counter, you happen upon the photographs in your drawer of the two of you and all of a sudden, you're sobbing uncontrollably, never mind that the cat has to get to the vet and Junior is late for soccer practice and the sink just backed up—you can't even move.

Then there is the issue of "putting on a brave front" or any kind of front for that matter. There are a great many of you who feel like you have to pretend to the world that you're not hurting and that you're not grieving. I don't know when it became necessary for us to start hiding our feelings, but apparently, there's a lot of it going on out there and this needs to come to a halt as well. Putting on a front means that you're not allowing yourself the opportunity to grieve and as we have already learned, feelings that get avoided, put away or are hidden behind some kind of "front" will come back to "get you"—this is an absolute certainty.

The other problem with putting on a front is that if you don't make the time to grieve, you inevitably forget to take the front off. That "mask" of bravery that you're wearing becomes a permanent fixture. Now, since I'm fluent in the language of makeup and cosmetics, let's look at this "bravery-mask-front" thing another way. Approximately 99.99999 percent of us wear some kind of makeup (and in my case, just about EVERY kind of makeup). What would happen if we never took off our makeup and just kept piling more makeup on top of the old—day after day, week after week? The skin underneath would become pretty awful and makeup is only as good as the skin under it. Piled-on makeup makes you feel "icky" just thinking about it, doesn't it?

Now let's take a look at your putting on your brave "front", be it in front of your children, your parents, your work colleagues or the world at large. If you never take that front "off" in order to grieve and move through the pain, guess what? The soul underneath suffers. Pretty soon, in the interest of that "front" that you're so desperately trying to keep up, you're now ignoring your own emotional needs altogether—and then we have a whole new set of challenges with which to deal. Just like we take off the makeup and cleanse our faces to ensure healthy skin, it's now time to take off the "front" in order to cleanse our souls.

Remember, the one person on this entire planet that you cannot fool is you! So for those of you who have been very busy putting on a front and acting as though you're "over it" and bucking for your own Academy Award...

I want you to *stop* it.

I want you to drop the front, acknowledge just how miserable you're feeling at that moment and then decide at what time that day you're going to let yourself go and feel the really, really bad emotions you've been repressing.

Does compartmentalizing mean that you never think about how lousy you feel in the course of a day? Obviously not; that would come under the heading of trying to be Superwoman. What it does mean, however, is that you must learn to put it aside for now in the interest of whatever needs to be done at the moment. This could be anything from performing your 8-to-5 job to helping your children deal with their grief, to unclogging the sink, getting the cat to the vet and Junior to soccer practice!

I used to make a "deal" with myself every single day. When feelings of grief threatened to overcome me and there were tasks I needed to accomplish, I told myself, "Okay, I know you're feeling pretty rotten right now, but you also have to _____ (work, take Kendall to cheerleading practice, etc.) right now. However, you get to feel absolutely, completely, 100 percent miserable at 9:00 p.m.", or the particular hour at night where "day is done": work is over with, children's needs are taken care of and the house is quiet (which, for us, is generally at nighttime, when even our cats are quiet). Then I made sure that I kept that appointment with me. At this appointed hour, I soaked in a tub or enjoyed a cup of tea or glass of wine or read one of my "grief helper" books or listened to sad songs or cried my eyes out and railed at the world that my husband was not here. Nothing and no one distracted me from the very necessary activity of grieving.

People constantly ask, "Carole, after everything that you've been through (which is a similar experience to the one you're going through), how is it possible now to be so happy and positive and upbeat?" I believe it's because I literally gave myself permission every single day to take the time to feel totally rotten and by doing that, I was also able to—guess what— heal and move forward! I know that this is your ultimate goal as well and we are going to get you there!

## JUST FOR YOU

Now it's your turn. Set aside a time to allow yourself to grieve during the day or evening, and ask yourself what would be the best time to do so. When is your house quiet and at peace? Is it at night when the children are in bed or perhaps early in the morning when the sun is coming up and the day is new? Whatever your preferred time of day, make an appointment with yourself and *keep* it…NO EXCUSES! This is when you get to feel angry or overwhelmingly sad or just plain lousy, whatever it is that day that you are feeling. Setting the time aside for you on a daily basis, even if it's only twenty minutes, will otherwise throughout the day allow you to tell yourself, "I'm not feeling good right now, but I'm going to put this aside until (insert your grief-time here) and then I'll get to feel absolutely horrible."

Please note that Quiet Time does *not* include:

- Television.
- Telephones, cell phones, text messaging, BlackBerrys, Sidekicks, Palm Pilots or any other hi-tech devices or distractions.
- Returning emails, returning telephone calls, paying bills, grocery shopping, errand running, housecleaning, children's homework or anything that will otherwise distract you from you. These activities are called "creative avoidance" and I don't want you to avoid expressing your grief—creatively or otherwise.

As odd as this may sound, you will actually start to look forward to the time of day or night spent alone with you and your grief. Not only that, but also as you grow on and through your healing journey as you continue to take this time, you will notice that you spend less time grieving and more time "enjoying"—be it the bath, the sunrise, the tea or the book. When you learn to compartmentalize your life and your grief, you will find that you have loads of time and attention for everything and everyone—most especially, **YOU!**

## QUIET TIME "QUIZ AND COMMIT"

Get out your make-believe makeup case in your mind—how many "compartments" do you have? There's a compartment for work, a compartment for children, a compartment for children's activities, a compartment for your activities. Now we're going to include a compartment for grieving time that is yours alone. Grab your pen and let's create that compartment!

- At this point in my healing journey, my grief mostly takes form in the way of _____ (anger, crying at "inopportune times", inability to concentrate, lashing out, depression, etc.):

  _____

  _____

  _____

  _____

  _____

- Understanding that schedules are not always constant, my house is generally quiet and/or I have at least twenty to thirty minutes of uninterrupted time to myself in the _____ (morning, early to mid-afternoon, evening, late night).

- I will most enjoy engaging in the following activities during my Quiet Time. These will be activities that will help me focus on and deal with my grief by allowing me the freedom to feel just as badly as I choose to feel, without feeling guilty for doing so:

  _____

  _____

  _____

  _____

# CAROLE'S COMPLETELY NON-NEGOTIABLE COMPARTMENTALIZING CONTRACT

## I PROMISE, WITHOUT FAIL:

- I will set aside time each day for the sole purpose of feeling sad, depressed, angry or otherwise miserable, understanding that this is a normal, natural and vital part of the grieving process.
- I will not feel guilty for setting this specific time aside for me. This is not an act of greed or selfishness on my part. I am not neglecting anything or anyone by taking this time for me, and everything that I'm looking at that needs to be done still will be there waiting for me after my Quiet Time is finished.
- I understand that my personal Quiet Time will not involve any outside people or potentially distracting influences, such as the television, the telephone, the computer or any household responsibilities. I understand that this is the proper time for the acknowledgment of my loss and grief as well as the emotional renewal and strengthening of my spirit and my soul.
- I will recognize that each time I commit to taking this essential daily time for myself, I am traveling forward in a positive way on my healing journey. As I continue to move through each chapter in this book and with each day that passes, I am progressing further toward achieving a stronger spirit and a peaceful and healed heart.

### Chapter 4

# YOUR "HEALING TIMELINE" vs. EVERYONE ELSE'S "HEALING TIMELINE"

There are two distinct timelines in widowhood: your personal "healing timeline" and the "healing timeline" of the "person" we'll call "Everyone Else".

Everyone Else tells you when to start getting rid of your husband's clothes and that they're going to "help you" go through everything—whether or not you asked for help is of no consequence. Everyone Else lets you know that it's been way too long since you've gone out with them or gone out on a date or gone out period. Everyone Else tells you that saving his favorite bottle of cologne is stupid. Everyone Else tells you that you haven't taken enough time off work. Everyone Else tells you that it's time to get back to work. Everyone Else tells you that you're working too hard and that you're hiding from life in your work. Everyone Else lets you know that it's too soon to start dating, unless of course, you've waited too long to start dating. Everyone Else is telling you, "Enough time has passed; get over it already!" Everyone Else constantly lets you know, "It's what *he* would have wanted." Mind you that "it" will be many different things, but whatever "it" is, your husband would have wanted it!

Everyone Else reminds you that you're a widow (because you need reminding, right?) and that it's "time" to take off your wedding rings; unless of course you've taken the rings off "too soon"—don't worry, Everyone Else will let you know. Everyone Else tells you that you're sleeping too much or you're not sleeping enough or that you're not eating enough or that you're eating too much and in any case, you're for sure not eating right. Everyone Else, somehow or another, becomes the all-knowing expert on the subject entitled, "You and Your Pain."

Guess what?

## EVERYONE ELSE DOESN'T HAVE A DAMN CLUE!

There, I said it.

To be fair, Everyone Else no doubt has your best interests—or what Everyone Else _believes_ to be your best interests—at heart. However, the only timeline that matters here is YOURS. Period. You are the only person who knows when it's "time" to go through his clothes or sell his car or put his pictures away or take off your wedding rings or make your return to work or socializing. You might be reading this not even being able to comprehend doing such things. That means IT'S NOT TIME...yet. Do not listen to Everyone Else, who is not living the experience called Your Life, in your house, with your children.

How do you know when it's time—for any of it? You will wake up one day and make the decision that it's time. You will have the absolute, without-a-doubt knowing that the time has arrived. Sounds simple and perhaps even a little stupid, but it happens just like that. If you have children, no one had to tell you that you were in labor the first time; you just knew it. Same rules apply here.

In the days and weeks immediately following Mike's death, I didn't want to get rid of anything with which he ever came into contact. I wanted to keep everything that he touched, wore, sat on, laid in, commented on, loved or hated. Then one day, inexplicably, I knew that it was time to go into the closet and take his clothes out. Another day, I realized it was time to take down his many awards and accolades and put them away. Still another day, it was time to donate his favorite chair (I'm fairly certain that all men have one of those!). All of these activities took place over a period of many months, not days, and certainly not anytime soon after his death. With time came the absolute knowledge of what should be kept, what should be passed along as heirloom and what needed to be either donated or disposed of.

## CRY AND CARRY ON

Are you finding it too difficult to part with certain things? Then *don't part with them*—how simple is that?

One particular dilemma that I experienced was in going through Mike's shirts. Mike was an "old-school" cowboy, you see, and had fifty-three (yes, fifty-three) absolutely beautiful western-style shirts that I could not bear to simply "give away"—we should all have in the bank what was in that closet in western shirts alone!

Despite my altruistic nature and the fact that I wholeheartedly support several charities, the thought of donating Mike's shirts—which were such an integral part of his persona—made me weep. On the other hand, I knew that it was completely impractical to hold on to fifty-three shirts. I came up with what I believe to be a wonderful idea—I cut a square from each shirt and I had the squares made into a quilted wall hanging that will be passed on to Kendall and subsequently on to her children.

You keep whatever it is that brings you peace, joy, comfort or whatever it is that you seek (if the item(s) is not otherwise specifically addressed in your husband's will).

---

### FROM THE STILETTO FILE

Anything that you do decide to donate to charity is tax deductible. Be sure to itemize carefully, since the Internal Revenue Service will generally request itemization of things cumulatively valued over $500.00.

---

## No "Help Wanted"

Though I had many offers from family and close friends to help me "go through" Mike's things, I declined each and every offer. For me, this was a very personal part of the healing journey that I had to make on my own as a new widow. I wanted to keep that part of our life—and that part of my heart—private. I wanted to take the time to reminisce over cowboy boots, old greeting cards that we had exchanged over the years, those cologne bottles, well-worn paperbacks, silly New Year's Eve photographs and Super Bowl Sunday "Supersonic Chili" recipes without having to worry about crying or laughing or potentially offending Everyone Else, because they might disagree with what I was either keeping or passing along. This may sound very selfish—however, at this very difficult time in your life, you need to reserve the right to be a little selfish.

Making decisions on getting rid of, keeping or giving away his things is truly about you right now. This is your healing journey. If you feel like having one or two friends or family members help you or a household full of people help you with the "go through" process, by all means do so; particularly if it will make the process easier or give you additional support or comfort. However, if you are feeling as I did, then this is something that you need to keep to yourself. You must know that it's fine to feel this way. Don't have a problem letting people know that this is something that you must do on your own—all alone.

## "It's" What He Would Have Wanted—Whatever "It" Is (Plus, What He Really Wanted)

Let's go over one of the myths that may be causing you concern, guilt or pain. It's the one which goes you have absolutely no idea how much your husband wanted, until Everyone Else lets you know! Even more remarkable is the fact that in many instances, Everyone Else didn't even know your husband, yet Everyone Else is perfectly aware of what he did or did not want:

- "You have to start going out again; it's what he would have wanted."
- "You need to get back to work; it's what he wanted you to do."
- "You can't spend all of your time grieving; he did not want you to do that!"

You get the general idea.

Sometimes, out of genuine concern, people will give you a laundry list of what your husband "wanted". Sometimes the hurt inflicted is unintentional, but occasionally this approach is oftentimes nothing more than a manipulative ploy. When people said these things to me, I unfortunately believed them; especially when I might not have been performing as well as I should have at work, when I chose to keep certain items of Mike's rather than dispose of them (or vice versa), when I made decisions as to how to run my life or raise my daughter. I constantly ran into these editorial comments as to what my husband "wanted". Of course, when I fell short of Everyone Else's expectations, I naturally felt guilty, because in my mind, I didn't accomplish "what Mike would have wanted."

It took me a while before I remembered that Mike and I had a little over two years prior to his death to discuss in great detail *exactly* what he wanted. Drawing on that experience, now I am going to save you much time and worry over listening to others tell you what your husband wanted. Despite what anyone may tell you and even though chances are excellent that I did not know your husband personally, I *do* know what your husband wanted for you. Ready?

Drum roll please…

Your husband wanted you (and your children) to be:

- **Healthy**
- **Happy**
- **At peace**

That's it.

This is what your husband wanted for you and your family. He neither "wanted" nor expected you to quit grieving within a week, immediately return to peak performance at your job or anything else that others may "frame", using what he "wanted" as a tactic to get what they may want, need or expect from you.

No one knew your husband as well as you did in the way that you did. In your heart, you know exactly what he wanted for you. Empower yourself with that knowledge and with the love that you carry for your husband in your heart—as well as the love that he carried for you. Please do not allow others to goad you into doing things for which you are not ready under the guise of, "It's what he would have wanted." No it isn't. It's perfectly fine to go ahead and skip all of the guilt and anguish that you might otherwise experience if you allow others to cause you to second-guess yourself and stay up nights wondering, "What does he want me to do?" You already know what he wanted. You may rest comfortably in the peace of that knowledge.

## "I'm Getting You Out of Here."

Here comes well-meaning Everyone Else again.

Everyone Else has now decided that you need to go out; despite how you may be feeling. This may be a few days after the death or funeral, perhaps a week or two. At some point, Everyone Else will pop up and try to make the decision for you that it's time for you to be social. Sometimes, Everyone Else will even phrase it as a "threat"; as in, "If I don't hear from you by (thus-and-such deadline), I'm coming to get you." Now you feel like you "have" to go out to please Everyone Else.

My advice is:

Only if you want to.

I initially limited my goings-out to pie and coffee or a movie with

Kendall and that was fine for me. As with everything else on this new journey, this too was a "baby-step" process. Little by little, I began to feel up to socializing again. As you can see, you cannot be afraid to "hurt" feelings. When Everyone Else begins to insist that it's "time" for you to resume socializing, state quietly but firmly that you are not quite ready for "public or people" yet, but that as soon as you are, you will be sure to give them a call.

You must also bear in mind that going out into the world generally means that you will be discussing your husband, his last days, his death, the funeral, the catering, the flowers and the entire experience *over and over again*! This takes strength and that strength comes with time—which you must be willing to give yourself and you will need to insist that others give you as well.

## The "Lifting" Power of People

As you further progress into this book, you will discover that I am the quintessential People Person. However, even a People Person may have the tendency to "push" others away during a time of intense grief and I was no exception.

You have no doubt surmised by now that I am a huge proponent of the truism: "your timeline is the only one that matters." However, Everyone Else does have one need as well—the need to put their collective "arms" around you to show their love and support. This is as much a need for them to be allowed to comfort you as it is for you to permit the comfort to be given.

Almost immediately after Mike's death, I was scheduled to attend a business conference in Dallas, consisting of about 10,000 other attendees. These conferences are always filled with excitement, enthusiasm, recognition and applause; for me, it's always a wonderfully fun time. However, this time I had scarcely finished with Mike's funeral, so as you can well imagine, this conference was obviously the very last thing of which I wanted to be a part of at that moment in time. At that point, I really was not even up to getting out of my pajamas, let alone going to a conference and making a feeble attempt at being "celebratory".

I was resolute in my decision not to attend when I received a call from a colleague who was not only an amazing mentor and inspiration to me, but she also was very much a part of our family's journey throughout Mike's illness. She called me to her office in an effort to persuade me to attend the conference. Others had tried and failed before her and this phone call was not going to dissuade me from my resolute decision to stay at home, in my pajamas, with the blinds shut. After patiently listening to my protests, and with more patience than I would have had with me, she said, "Carole, there are so many people who want to put their arms around you and share in your sorrow. Please come and allow us to lift you."

I never did win many arguments with her.

It was at that moment when I realized that those who cared for me and who were such integral parts of our family's journey through Mike's illness also needed to be able to show their love and support. It would have been selfish for me to deny those who truly cared about my welfare the opportunity to share their sympathies.

I did go to that conference and although I was naturally subdued and there was more crying than laughing on my part, I am so very grateful that I made the choice to allow others "in". Left to my own devices, I would have stayed home in those pajamas with the blinds shut.

You may not yet be at the point of "socializing" and I wholeheartedly support that decision. However, I sincerely suggest as soon as you can to allow people the opportunity to "lift" you. It doesn't have to be at a conference with thousands of people…if you work outside the home and have, since your husband's death, returned to your job, go to lunch or coffee with your colleagues. If you are a stay-at-home mom, have your best girlfriend or your neighbor in to share a cup of tea. You need the support and the reinforcement and those in your life need to be able to offer it. Don't push it or them away.

## Ring Around The…

As with going through and/or the disposition of your late husband's belongings, the decision as to the eventual removal of your wedding rings is a difficult and heart-wrenching decision indeed. Like everything else about this experience, it hurts; plain and simple. There is also the potential for guilt at "declaring" to the world that you are no longer married. Of all of the timelines and the "when-to's", this may very well be the most intensely personal and in the thousands of letters that I receive every month, it is also one of the questions that I am asked most frequently.

Some widows remove their wedding rings immediately. Others never remove them at all, for the rest of their lives. In my case, I chose again to take "baby steps". Several months into my healing journey, I moved my wedding rings to my right hand. Even though I felt that I was moving forward with my life, wearing the rings on my right hand continued to provide me with comfort and I didn't feel quite as "naked" as I would have, had I not been wearing the rings at all. I wore my rings on my right hand for roughly three years after Mike's passing (yes, even after I started dating and subsequently became seriously involved with a man). It was only when I was ready and when I felt comfortable that I made the decision to remove my rings. Those precious rings are now put away for Kendall, along with Mike's wedding ring.

As with all of the other timelines we have discussed and will be discussing, I do not believe that there is a "right" or "wrong" regarding your rings. This decision will and must ultimately be yours. However, you will want to bear in mind that:

1. Should you eventually meet someone new, the presence of wedding rings on your left hand may become a touchy issue at some point—a new man may think that you have been unable to "say goodbye" and are unable to move forward from your husband's death. Just as your new companion will need to be very sensitive to your feelings and justification(s) behind your continuing to wear your rings, so then you must be sensitive to his feelings as well. You'll discover more about this issue when we discuss the "Ghost of Husband Past" in chapter 10.

2. If your engagement and/or wedding rings were heirlooms from your husband's side of the family, it might be appropriate to at

least make the offer to return the rings to his family. They may likely refuse the jewelry, but I believe it to be the proper and kind gesture to make.

Other than these two considerations, if wearing your rings brings you peace, comfort, joy or whatever it is that you seek as you progress on your healing journey (and as you've already learned, it is _your_ healing journey), you wear those rings despite what Everyone—or _Anyone_—Else says or thinks!

## The Best Decision is No Decision—Yet

There are then the widows who react to death in a completely opposite manner. Rather than wanting to hang onto everything, they want to dispose of absolutely everything immediately—sometimes as quickly as a week or two after the death. Just as is the instinct to hold onto everything tightly, this too is a severe reaction to death and grief. Within the first few weeks and months after your husband's death, it is my absolute strongest recommendation that you:

• Do not make any major financial decisions right now. This includes moving away from and/or the sale of your home.

In the movie _Sleepless in Seattle_, Tom Hanks' character relocates himself and his young son from Chicago to Seattle almost immediately after his wife's death. He does this in an effort to escape feeling like he's going to "see" his late wife "every time I turn a corner." While this makes for the beginnings of an excellent plot in an excellent movie, it is not a wise move to make in the real everyday world.

I know too well how hard it is to be expecting your husband to be around "every single corner" in your home and in your daily life. I wistfully recall expecting to hear that slam of the front door, listening for that wonderfully familiar booming voice from the living room or expecting to see him playing peek-a-boo around the corner into the kitchen as I prepared dinner. However, as difficult as all of this is, please don't be in a hurry to get out of your house permanently or do anything of a financial nature that could potentially jeopardize your economic future. Consult with your accountant or a financial expert before you do anything of a financial nature. The exceptions to this would be the need for immediate generation of income to you and your family on a regular basis and/or acting in accordance with the last will and testament of your husband, both of which should be done as soon as is reasonably possible.

• Do not dramatically change the cut or color of your hair. The same holds for surgically altering your appearance (and that includes tattoos or piercing anything).

Do not do anything to radically alter your appearance; at least not right now. Instead, treat yourself to a makeover with cosmetics (which washes off if you don't like it), a new outfit or two (which can be returned if you don't like them) or a professional massage and pedicure (which I recommend anyway). You can treat yourself to "freshening up and feeling better" without doing something with permanent (or in the case of your hair, *seemingly* permanent!) consequences.

• Do not quit your job or change careers at this time.

Again, the instinct may be to get rid of and change everything all at once, particularly if you are not especially happy with your current job or career. For now though, it's better to adhere to a known routine which you know and with which you feel comfortable. There has been enough upheaval in your life and human beings can absorb only so many traumas at one time. Staying in your present career for the time being will allow you to take comfort in and enjoy the security of the day-to-day schedule you're accustomed to. Once you are further along in your healing processes, you will be able to focus your attention and energy, if you make the decision, on finding a new job or new career or direction—for that's a big change as well. You will also know that you are making the change for actual, rather than "reactionary", reasons.

## WIDOWS WEAR STILETTOS "HEART MONITOR"

Who is the Everyone Else in your life? It's now time to look at how you are best going to deal with the opinions, observations and influences of those around you.

Has anyone made "suggestions" to you or rendered opinion(s) as to how you should be coping in general with your husband's death? Who is the Everyone Else in your life? List your Top Five:

_____

_____

_____

_____

_____

What are some of the suggestions or observations that Everyone Else has made to you? In one word, how did each one of these suggestions *initially* make you feel? Rushed? Angry? Misunderstood? Be absolutely 100 percent honest with yourself, remembering that however you felt at that moment is perfectly okay!

The suggestion that was made was that I should:

_____

When I heard it, I felt:

_____

The suggestion that was made was that I should:

_____

When I heard it, I felt:

_____

The suggestion that was made was that I should:

_____

When I heard it, I felt:

_____

The suggestion that was made was that I should:

_____

When I heard it, I felt:

_____

Has Everyone Else offered to help you with the "go through" process of your husband's things? If so, how did you respond—and how did you *want* to respond?

_____
_____
_____
_____
_____

Let's talk about your wedding rings. Write about this issue today; revisit your thoughts again in six months and then again in one year.
Today's date:_____

Despite what Everyone Else is telling me or may tell me, when it comes to my rings, I *really* want to:

_____
_____
_____
_____
_____

---

### CAROLE'S "COMEBACK CORNER"

When Everyone Else makes suggestions as to what you should or should not be doing or how you should or should not be feeling, you may choose to respond:

**"Everyone Else, I SO appreciate your (idea, opinion, suggestion) and I know that you want the best for me. I'm handling (the situation that's inviting the suggestion) in my own way and my own time and it's working just fine for me."**

When Everyone Else volunteers to help go through your husband's things with you, should you prefer not to have assistance, you may choose to respond:

**"Everyone Else, it's so nice of you to want to help me out— but this is something that I really need to do all by myself. I'd love to see you later on though [only if you really want to]. When can we get together?"**

---

## MAKE A NOTE ON YOUR CALENDAR TO COME BACK TO THIS PAGE SIX MONTHS FROM TODAY'S DATE

How do you feel about your wedding rings today?

Today's date:_____

Despite what Everyone Else is telling me or may tell me, when it comes to my rings, I *really* want to:

_____

_____

_____

_____

_____

_____

## MAKE A NOTE ON YOUR CALENDAR TO COME BACK TO THIS PAGE SIX MONTHS FROM TODAY'S DATE

Let's check in one more time and see how you're feeling about your wedding rings after a year.

How do you feel about your rings today?

Today's date:_____

Despite what Everyone Else is telling me or may tell me, when it comes to my rings, I *really* want to:

_____

_____

_____

_____

Now, look back at the last year. Have you progressed in your feelings regarding your rings? If you don't feel that you've at all progressed, remember that, as we learned in this chapter, it simply means that it's not "time"… yet! Continue to "check in" with you every six months to see how you feel about this very personal decision—and please remember that the definition of "personal decision" means that the decision is *yours alone!*

### JUST FOR YOU

I do recognize that, to you, I am yet another "Everyone Else"; telling you what to do and how to do it. Though my advice and insight does come from direct experience, I also encourage you to remember, first and foremost, that this is YOUR timeline, not Everyone Else's timeline. This is a new and unknown world for you and only YOU will know when any time is the "right" time, although you may not have a great deal of faith in your judgment right now. I have always believed in listening carefully to that little voice deep down inside of all of us—that voice will not lead you astray. Listen to yourself and trust in yourself! Take a good look at that "girl in the mirror": she is strong, she is smart and she is making strides through this life-altering challenge!

And speaking of that "girl" in the mirror…

### Chapter 5

# WHO IS THAT "GIRL" IN THE MIRROR?

**(And How to Find You Again)**

Fashion, diet and exercise are integral parts of our lives and our societal conscience, perhaps more now that ever before.

I happen to know, without reservation, that as a new young widow, you don't really care about any of it, much less how you *yourself* look or feel.

There are several rational reasons behind your line of thinking:

- Clothes? As long as it covers you up in public and the local Health Department doesn't come a-calling, what difference does it make?

- Exercise? If it was a challenge to find the time, energy and motivation to exercise before the passing of your beloved, it's virtually impossible to find any of it right now, not that you've looked recently.

- Diet? Who cares? The kids are fed and you're either not hungry at all or you've made a steady diet out of whatever takes less than three-and-a-half minutes; either in the microwave or at the drive-thru.

- You are too tired or depressed or sad (or all three) to care much about what you look like, what you're wearing, what you're eating or how you're taking care of yourself—if in fact, you're taking care of yourself at all.

It certainly doesn't help us as widows that everywhere we turn we are besieged by fashion, diet and exercise. Designers clamor for our attention and our wallet contents; magazines and cable television channels are dedicated solely to the pursuit of shopping. Sunglasses have never mattered quite as much as they do today and of course, don't even get me started on shoes, my personal Achilles Heel, no pun intended!

Exercise. It seems like every five minutes there's a hot new workout/gym gimmick or video promising us a rock-hard-this or a perky-that. Dieting clearly has become the new Great American Pastime: diet books, diets online, diet foods, diet plans, diet drinks, diet classes, diet gurus, diet counseling. There's a reason that it's a ten billion dollar-a-year industry and that reason is us!

I know what you're thinking: who's around to care? Since your husband isn't here anymore, there's no one for whom to dress up and nowhere to go and you're not interested in impressing anyone else or going anywhere anyway. So there's no point in even caring what your body's like, how you feel, what you do or don't eat or what you look like, right?

Not entirely.

At the heart of it all is this fact: we are women. Even better, we are all girls, be it the Divas or the Tomboys. The reality is that we want to look good and we want to feel good. Regardless of how awful you might feel right this moment, I know that you want to return to that feeling of "fresh and fabulous" or "spunky and sassy" or maybe just "here and human." I'm here to help you do it—little by little, step by step.

## Get Out of Your Sweats—Get Into Your Clothes!

We all know that when we look good, we feel better. I know that you feel differently about yourself when you're dressed nicely than when you're wearing your torn flannel pajamas with the feet in them. Problem is, since you've become a widow you haven't had the time or inclination to pay any real attention to yourself. You don't even realize how neglected you've been. Please be aware that feeling this way has happened on every young widow's journey; regardless of whether you consider yourself to be a "fashionista" or a "fashion-not-so-much".

Prior to Mike's illness, ours was, honestly speaking, a wonderfully upbeat and very social life. It seemed like we were constantly "on-the-go"—weddings, formal dinner-dances and, of course, getting all dressed up just to go out and have a good time. Going one step further, for me, half the fun of going out was the getting-ready-to-go-out process (or what I laughingly refer to as "urban renewal").

Once Mike became ill, life changed dramatically. As is typical for the life of a caregiver to an ill spouse, my life during Mike's illness was limited chiefly to work, caring for Mike and the two of us as parents together, making sure that our daughter Kendall's daily routine remained as "normal" as possible under the most challenging set of circumstances. Any time spent away from home involved only work (which I did in a suit), grocery shopping (which I did in old, yucky, oversized sweats) and taking Kendall to and picking her up from school and her activities (in the same beautiful sweats).

Time dragged during the period after Mike's death. I had little enthusiasm or energy and barely got through the necessities of life. One night, Kendall thought it a good idea that we get out of the house for an evening and suggested that we go to a movie. I didn't much feel like going anywhere, but I knew that Kendall needed to feel like she was "helping Mommy" by getting us both out of the house. So despite wanting to stay home, I quickly pulled on my good old several-sizes-too-big sweats (these things were truly hideous), ran a brush through my hair and grabbed my purse—I think the entire getting-ready ritual took a grand total of ten minutes. As we were preparing to leave the house, Kendall looked me up and down with a grimace on her face and said, "You're not going to wear *that*, are you?"

Honestly, I didn't even stop to think what I had done or rather, *hadn't* done. The fact was that it had been so long since I had gotten "dressed up" to go out somewhere, it never occurred to me to take the time to look good as I did when my husband was still alive and start doing so now.

Kendall then very lovingly took me by the hand, led me back into my room and selected an outfit consisting of low-rise jeans, black high-heeled boots, a black angora sweater and black leather jacket for me to wear. I protested feebly, saying that we were "only" going to the movies—the "Who's Going to Care" defense. She wouldn't hear any of my excuses, saying, "Mom, it's time for you to 'get dressed' again."

*Out of the mouths of babes…*

It was one of the very first epiphanies that I had in my new life as a young widow: that the only difference between a rut and the grave is the size of the hole—and I had dealt with graves quite enough, thank you. However, without even realizing it, I was standing in a great big rut in my great big sweats. Let's face it, that's how most ruts happen—no one goes out of their way to get into a rut; yet we wake up one day and there we are, waist deep in Bad Habit Land. The great news is that we also have the ability to pull ourselves right up out of there!

So after two and a half years, I took off (and threw away) the gargantuan sweats, put on the outfit that Kendall selected, put on makeup just like I used to, climbed back into those high-heeled boots that had been languishing for so long and made my entrée back into life as a girl.

And you know what? It felt fantastic.

It has nothing to do with how much or how little of a "dressing-up" person you are; the fact is that when you put yourself together, you feel awesome. When your hair looks amazing, when your skin is glowing and your makeup looks great, when you have on your favorite jeans or dress or whatever outfit makes you feel like taking on the world, your attitude completely changes. And you are *so* entitled to a change of attitude!

I'm betting that you haven't had much of a reason to get dressed up for anything lately—or even much felt like it. That's okay; I'm not saying that it's time to go find a New Year's party, but the next time you go to a movie or a restaurant or even for coffee, try this: put on something that you love, maybe something that you haven't worn in a long while—a favorite pair of jeans with a frilly blouse or a fun t-shirt and great blazer; a gorgeous piece of jewelry; the fabulous shoes that everyone envies; your cute hat or your vintage earrings. You can do this even if—or maybe *especially* if—you are a stay-at-home parent and going out consists of trips to the park with the kids; you do NOT get to use your career as a mother as an excuse for neglecting YOU!

## Fashion Forward—or Fashion Flub?

When it comes to fashion, I have always been an "envelope pusher" (well, actually, an envelope shredder!).

Loosely translated, this means that I have always loved expressing my feelings, my emotions and my excitement for life through fashion—plus I *hate* looking like everyone else. Fashion, quite simply, is fun and it is wonderful when you have reached the point in your recovery when you are ready to return to the "fun" of fashion.

That said, I am also a huge advocate of the following very wise and time-honored "rules" of fashion:

* Know Your Limitations.

Do I believe that once a woman is over twenty-two years of age that she has to "cover up" from head to toe? Absolutely not—and I'm offended by any so-called "fashion experts" who say that we do. Many of my contemporaries in their forties look better now than they did when they were in their twenties and there's no reason not to enjoy that fact.

Does it mean that you have to be a size negative four to enjoy fashion? That's a straight-out-loud NO! Look around you—designers have finally started paying attention to the fact that women are built like women. Nowadays, women of all sizes and shapes can enjoy all of the fun of fashion without breaking the bank or feeling like they have to "hide" in anything "big, baggy and balloon-like" if they are not a single-digit size.

On the other hand, are there trends that I choose to skip? Definitely. For example, while I might wear a short skirt, it will not be plaid or covered with ruffles or pleats. Anything "baby doll" or "short puffy sleeved" or too "cutesy" is something else that I avoid. I do wear low-rise jeans as this is the most flattering cut for my body type; however, I can also sit confidently in them without everyone around me knowing the size, color, style and brand of my underpinnings. Showing off a sliver of tummy in the summertime is fine (especially after all those abdominal crunches, right?); however, showing tummy enough to rival that of a pubescent pop star is not.

In other words—know your limitations and work within those limitations. It's easy to do!

Fashion hasn't been this exciting or all-encompassing in years. Hemlines for pants *and* skirts are all over the place, as are heel heights. You can be anything from comfy-casual to "boho-chic" to city-sophisticate to "country-cutie", regardless of age or body-type. There are more than enough trends of which we can all happily take advantage.

But please, ladies, legwarmers belong in the gym—and no ruffled bobby socks with high heels. *Ever.*

- Know Your Strong Suits.

Too often, we spend so much time staring in the mirror at everything that is *wrong*, we forget to emphasize what we have that is wonderful! Just as we recognize our limitations, so we should also know our strong points and play them up. For example, do you have gloriously long, thick hair? Huge eyes? How about a swan-like neck or a gorgeous back or super-shapely legs?

Take a good, long, *objective* look at yourself. Beauty is *not* about the number on the scale or the digit-size on the label in your clothes (neither of which anyone sees anyway!). Take a serious look at yourself, figure out what it is about you that you'd love to emphasize and then do it! For example, play up your huge eyes with wonderful makeup that brings them out. A long neck is perfect for chokers and "collar" style necklaces. Shapely legs are flattered by above-the-knee skirts and naturally, an *awesome* pair of shoes. Draw attention to the features about which you feel the most confident.

And not to be cliché, but the best strong suit that everyone has is a knockout smile.

- A Little Goes a Long Way.

Avoid wearing a "whole bunch of trendy" at the same time. For example, a pair of leopard print pumps with matching earrings and a black belted shirtdress looks awesome. On the other hand, wearing leopard print pumps with a leopard print bag and a leopard print pair of pants with a leopard print blazer and leopard print earrings will make you look like you were attacked at a wild animal park and lost the battle.

The same holds true for accessories. Decide what the focal point is going to be on your body. If you are wearing "shoulder sweeper" or "chandelier" earrings, leave the necklace off. If a dress or top has shiny or sparkly straps, wear small earrings and again, no necklace. If you are wearing very elaborately jeweled high-heeled sandals, don't wear a sequined belt and jeweled bracelet and necklace and earrings and rhinestone hairclip or you'll look like the Christmas tree at Rockefeller Center. Coco Chanel herself originated the phrase, "Before you leave the house, look at yourself in the mirror and take off one accessory." She wasn't wrong.

- Display Only "One End at a Time."

If you're like me and you're one of those women who likes to "turn it out" once in awhile, you likely haven't had the opportunity to do so in a long time. Maybe a special occasion or a "Girls' Night Out" is coming up and you get to once again dress up and go out and be girly. Good for you! As tempting as it may be to do otherwise though, please remember a cardinal rule of fashion: "one end at a time."

If you are wearing a fantastic mini skirt and high heels, cover up the cleavage. If you are wearing a "down to there" top, pair it with an awesome pair of jeans and spiky heels. If the short skirt/low cut top is an ensemble, throw a gorgeous blazer or "shrug" over it. Don't display it all at once—pick *one* focal point.

You have every right to "get out of your sweats" or whatever clothing in which you have been hiding and you have allowed to take the place of "dressing". You even have the right to look and feel beautiful. It's time. It's your turn. Grab a couple of fashion magazines (there are approximately one million of them out on the newsstands at any given moment), get some great ideas and GET DRESSED!

## Working "9 to 5"...Again

The death of your husband has brought many changes to your life; not the least of which may be the necessity of returning to work outside of the home to support your family. Between the advent of new and constantly-changing technologies with which you may be unfamiliar, coupled with the fact that you may have been "out of the game" for a while, the workplace remains a competitive arena.

Let's get you ready to get back out there!

After making sure that you have a fabulous résumé and after landing that all-important interview appointment, it's time to put your very best foot forward (in amazing shoes, of course). Whether you have been out of the workplace for a short time or a long while, it never hurts to go over the "fashion rules" of the interview to which one should adhere:

• Be familiar with the appropriate dress in the field in which you seek employment and dress accordingly for the interview. For example, if you are applying for jobs in the areas of finance or law, your manner of dress must be conservative, regardless of how you may dress outside of work. For this kind of interview, your best bet is a skirt-suit or dress, pantyhose (no matter where you live or the weather outside!) and closed toe pumps. Your hairstyle and make-up should also be on the conservative side and jewelry should be minimal (no dangly or sparkly earrings, jingle-jangle bracelets or huge "centerpiece" necklaces). Manicures should be conservative; save the flaming-red or black-satin nail polish for your toes. Also, when seeking employment in these fields, although you'll likely be able to wear pants once you land a position, I advise against showing up in pants for the interview...and never ever wear jeans!

• If you are seeking employment in the more "creative" fields, such as fashion, advertising, beauty or the arts, your dress may be on the slightly trendier side. For example, here is where a pair of really nice jeans and a fabulous blazer might be appropriate. However, regardless of whatever current denim trends exist, no jeans with holes, rhinestones, sequins, bleaching, etc., are appropriate for an interview; a dark wash or black denim is best.

• Please do not confuse "trendy" with "sexy" when dressing for any interview. In other words, cleavages and tummies need to be concealed. And while wearing an above-the-knee dress or skirt with a spiky or wedge heel might be acceptable in some places, wearing five-inch, clear-heeled, furry platforms and a skirt so short that it becomes a belt when you sit down is not.

• Your purse should look like a purse and not like an overnight bag or an airline carry-on. You are there for an interview—you're not moving in. Also, avoid carrying purses that are clearly evening bags (bejeweled or rhinestone encrusted) and please leave backpacks, purses worn about the waist (sometimes referred to as "fanny packs" in the United States) and/or anything in the shape of an animal, fruit, vegetable or any other "novelty" to your children or for your weekend pleasure.

## Icing on the Cake

We're going to use the same principles for hair and makeup that we did with your clothes. Whether you are a "Diva Goddess" (like me) and love makeup and never met a hair product that you didn't love (or at least tried) or you are a "Back to Basics Girl" and keep it to mascara and lip gloss and a hairstyle that's "blow and go", now's the time to assert your style, ladies! Your re-emergence includes caring for yourself once again and even though I do believe that beauty begins on the inside, since most people don't see your insides, you need to let it SHINE on the outside as well.

## "Hair-tastic" Advice

As advised earlier and for the time being, I do not recommend going from brunette beauty to blonde bombshell (or the opposite), chopping six inches off your hair or otherwise doing anything that is so overly drastic that it will cause you to look in the mirror, cry and ask yourself if you inadvertently ate paint chips while deciding on this hair faux pas. Wait just a little while until you are certain that you are clearer of mind and are making a hairstyle decision for all of the right reasons. Simply maintain the hairstyle that you have for now and if you want to "mix it up" a little bit, you can do something as simple as trying a new shampoo, or something fun like purchasing an inexpensive, cool hairpiece or extension—they are EVERYWHERE nowadays!

Consult fashion and hairstyle magazines, visit a trusted stylist for his or her opinion and always remember Carole's Primary Law of Hair:

---

### CAROLE'S PRIMARY LAW OF HAIR

Hair grows back at the rate of ¼ inch per month;
unless you've chopped it all off and hate it.
In which case, the rate of hair growth
slows to ¼ inch per year.

---

### FROM THE STILETTO FILE

Hairpieces and extensions aren't just for celebrities and you don't have to pay celebrity prices to get them! Available in just about every color and in all styles, from ponytails to up-do's to "down-to-there" clip-on extensions, these wonderful inventions allow you to make a temporary change—or at the very least, help you get through a really bad hair day!

## Makeup...It Isn't Just For Holidays Anymore!

As you have no doubt surmised by now, I love makeup. Always have—always will. All kinds for all occasions. It's no accident that I spent many successful years in the beauty and fashion industry...let's face it, I was earning a living by teaching skin care, using skin care, wearing makeup, teaching about makeup, talking about makeup and trying out new makeup. It is a fact that I have always been and always will be a heavy contributor to the economic welfare that is the multi-billion dollar cosmetics industry.

Makeup and good skin care are also the easiest things to forgo during a time of grief. Unlike going without clothing, you won't get arrested if you leave the house without makeup; no one will point and stare at you if you're not wearing eye shadow or lipstick; no one will criticize you for forgetting foundation or concealer and good old "soap and water" will get your face clean, right?

But you'll know the difference—and you'll certainly feel the difference!

I firmly believe that every woman can benefit from even the littlest bit of makeup—a touch of mascara or blush; a little bit of clear lip gloss. You don't have to wear three different eyeshadows and two different kinds of blush; just wear whatever makes you feel polished. Not a makeup expert? There is so much help available to you; from books and magazines to makeover experts and much of this help is absolutely free! Even if you aren't entirely comfortable with the finished results of a makeover, the process is fun, it's a well-deserved pampering and if worse comes to worse and you wind up hating it, everything washes off!

Remember too, makeup looks only as good as the skin under it! Be sure to take good care of your skin (and not with "just soap and water!). This means a cleansing, moisturizing and exfoliation regimen appropriate to your skin type. It does NOT have to be expensive or time-consuming; it just has to be suitable to your skin type. Round out your skin care by drinking lots of water, eating tons of green, leafy veggies and, above all, wearing sunscreen!

## The Biggest Beauty Secret...

...is one of my **favorite** beauty secrets...ready?

SLEEP!

As with multitasking, we have somehow become a society that also brags about how little sleep on which we either can or must function. When or why this became fashionable, I do not know; however, it is a trend in which I stubbornly refuse to participate. I do know that all the makeup and cosmetics and "revolutionary" skin care in the world won't fix tired! Not only that, lack of sleep will radically impact your immune system, which has already been compromised by fighting the heavy stress factors in your life at this moment in time when you are beset by the new responsibilities, tasks and cares of widowhood.

Of course, the irony here is that though you desperately need it, sleep is probably the most elusive element in your life right now. There's the emotional part of course—that big "hole" in the bed next to you and there's no denying that it's awful getting used to that hole. Then there's all of the "have-to's" that are in your head—from shopping lists to dental appointments to all of those thank you notes from the funeral—and let's not forget work. Sleep? I must be kidding, of course.

So let's get you some of that well-deserved rest. Some tried-and-true suggestions are:

1. "Empty the garbage"—that's the "to-do" list spinning around in your head. Write down everything that you need to accomplish the following day, in order of importance. When it's out of your mind and down on paper, you will suddenly feel like the most organized woman on the planet.

2. Any *decaffeinated* herbal tea; preferably one that contains chamomile or a chamomile blend, which has calming properties. So does warm milk (and no adding chocolate!).

3. A warm bath or shower using herbal blends or a lavender scent; also proven to calm the mind and body. Save your citrus or peppermint-y scents for the morning; these are energizing scents.

4. Journaling. As you are learning in this book, writing your feelings

out in "diary" form can be very therapeutic; it's not just for teenagers. This will also allow you to visually "see" your recovery in process!

5. A sleep mask. Don't laugh; these aren't just for the "pampered and privileged" and serious sleep masks don't look like they came from a socialite's garage sale. Not only does a sleep mask help block out light, it also psychologically sends the message to your mind that it's time to sleep. Sleep masks can be found quite inexpensively at drugstores and at discount retailers.

6. Soft, relaxing music. Save all exciting, energetic music for housecleaning or for laying on a beach someplace. Set a sleep timer, so that the radio or CD player will shut off by itself.

## FROM CAROLE'S JUKEBOX

Some of my personal favorite go-to-sleep music selections are:
1. The Brandenburg Concertos, Johann Sebastian Bach.
2. Anything New Age; "Soundscapes" or something that you might hear while at a spa. You can find these CDs at many places, from discount retailers to specialty bath and linen stores.
3 Any "smooth" (not fusion!) jazz.
4. Manheim Steamroller.
5. "The Four Seasons", Vivaldi.
6. Pachelbel's Canon in D Major.
7. Moonlight Sonata (all movements), Beethoven.

## CRY AND CARRY ON

Nighttime can be the most difficult period of the entire day right now—the hours can seem to stretch endlessly in front of you and you just can't seem to turn your mind off everything that's happened to you. If you have tried some of or all of these suggestions and you are still having difficulty sleeping at night, please speak to your medical doctor or a counselor, taking care to let her or him know that you have recently become a widow and the circumstances that you feel are causing the most difficulty.

### Chapter 6

# FUELING AND ENERGIZING

**(Diet and Exercise)**

Since I was an English major at college, I can't help but laugh at the "root" of the words "diet" and "exercise". The first three letters of "diet" are D-I-E and at the root of the word "exercise" is "exert".

Die and exert. Hmmm. Two words we do not have a lot of use for, especially right now.

So let's tweak our thinking a little bit. Instead of "diet", we're going to talk about "fueling" and instead of exercise, we're going to talk about "energizing".

## FOOD = FUELING

Confession time. As politically incorrect as this is to admit, I love fast food. Absolutely love it. In my world, French fries are the fifth food group. If I could be healthy and continue to maintain my current dress size and subsist completely on a diet consisting of fast food, macaroni and cheese (including the kind that comes in a box) and regular soda (not diet), I would be a very happy girl.

If I'm very quiet, I believe that I can hear my arteries slamming shut.

We all know that this is a completely impractical and unhealthy lifestyle, yet one into which we can easily slip. This is particularly true if you are a widow without children or you have one child; the rationale being, "It's just me" or "It's just the two of us." It's a lot faster and takes much less effort to run to the nearest French Fry Heaven or Pizza Palace than actually prepare a healthy meal at home.

However, to use a well-worn cliché, "You are What You Eat" or to be blunt, "Garbage In...Garbage Out." The one thing that you must particularly safeguard right now during this time of stress and challenge is your health. We know for a fact that stress is a major contributor to a reduced immune system; it is up to you to do all you can to boost your immune system. Our focus here has nothing to do with losing weight or gaining weight; this has to do with maintaining or, more importantly, regaining your health.

## "But I'm Not Hungry"

As we are well aware, loss of appetite is one of the major symptoms of depression. The thought of food can be overwhelming; yet without adequate nutrition, you are compromising your already-weakened immune system. Factor in the very heavy "hit" that your body has taken in the stress department and you have a recipe for all kinds of illnesses: viral, bacterial and stress-related.

Instead of trying to eat "three squares" a day (which are hard to manage under the best of circumstances), try mini-meals instead. Start out with instant oatmeal in the morning (small, manageable and healthy) and half a grapefruit with toast or crackers and cheese; then in two or three hours, have an apple or rice cakes with peanut butter. In another couple of hours, try a handful of almonds and a banana. Keep a bag of baby carrots in the refrigerator for snacks. Have a wonderful leafy salad and a chicken breast or grilled salmon in the evening. This way, you are fueling your body with good-for-you, easy-on-the-system foods and you're not being totally overwhelmed with the thought and/or sight of a whole bunch of delicious food.

## The "It's Just Me", "It's Only the Two of Us Now" (for those with one child), "I Don't Have Time" Excuses

Trust me, I was the master of two out of the three of those excuses—then I did my homework and found that mealtime does not have to be fancy or involve a lot of preparation time. For example, we do a lot of salads in our home and I purchase many salad items pre-cut and pre-washed, which saves a lot of time. I'm also now a big proponent of the "make ahead and freeze", so that we have things such as burger patties, beef stew, individual meat loaves and pasta dishes at the ready. My daughter and I are not huge breakfast eaters, so we keep a supply of instant oatmeal (the raisin-and-spice flavor tastes like oatmeal-raisin cookies!) as well as chocolate soy protein powder—when added to milk, it's like a chocolate shake. We also keep meal bars, meal replacement drinks and whole-grain cereal on our kitchen shelves. Even though we don't always succeed, we do our utmost to limit our "Fast Food Follies" to once a week. In addition, I always have my eye out for recipes in magazines, particularly those involving the words "quick and easy".

And guess what? When you eat at home, you save a TON of money!

Finally (and this is so simple), drink water! There are lots of different magic numbers as to how much water you "should" be drinking, but aim for at least 48 oz. of water a day. It doesn't have to be fancy. It doesn't have to be bottled. It just has to be water.

When you pay attention to your fueling and add water to the mix, you will be amazed at how much better you feel physically; not to mention how much better you will look. Your skin will positively glow, puffiness and dark circles in the eye area will diminish and your energy level will begin to return to normal. Please mind your "fueling" carefully so that your body will have what it needs to help you heal.

As with all other matters concerning health, if you have experienced a dramatic weight loss or gain, if you have experienced symptoms such as hair loss or any ongoing gastrointestinal difficulty, see your medical doctor immediately.

---

## FROM THE STILETTO FILE

Are you ready for some quick and easy recipe suggestions? The following are a few of our favorites and take just a little bit of time and effort.

---

## KENDALL'S DIJON-GINGER SALMON

This recipe was created by my daughter Kendall and is a family favorite, especially in the summertime.

> ½ lb. salmon filet
> 2 tbsp. fresh-grated ginger
> ¼ cup brown sugar
> 2 tbsp. Dijon mustard

Combine all ingredients except salmon. Poke salmon with fork all over and season with salt and pepper to preference. Brush sauce on fish prior to broiling. Broil for approximately ten minutes on each side or until cooked through. You may baste with additional sauce if desired. Use leftover sauce for dipping.

**GOES GREAT WITH**: Spanish rice and a green salad with balsamic vinaigrette dressing.

## CAROLE'S WORLD FAMOUS (okay, maybe not) TACO SALAD

A favorite at potluck parties and picnics.

> 2 lb. bag lettuce (iceberg is best for this salad)
> Green onion to preference, finely chopped
> 1 pkg. taco seasoning
> 1 lb. ground round (no more that 15 percent fat)
> (Note: you can also substitute 3 cups of cooked chicken for the beef.)
> 1 can kernel corn, drained
> 1 can black beans, drained
> 1 can diced tomatoes or diced tomatoes with green chilies, drained
> 1 cup mild cheddar cheese, grated

Ranch dressing (optional)
Tortilla chips, crumbled into large pieces (optional)

Place greens in large bowl. Brown ground round and drain. Add taco seasoning and cook according to package directions. Drain and set aside. Thoroughly drain all canned vegetables and combine with meat. Add to lettuce bowl and add cheese. Mix thoroughly. You may wish to add ranch dressing; however, the salad is so flavorful on its own that it really doesn't need additional dressing. Have the tortilla chips on the side to top off individual servings; if you add them to the salad and you have leftovers, the chips will get soggy.

**GOES GREAT WITH**: Steamed flour tortillas and a chilled glass of a really nice Chardonnay.

## "BAKED" SPAGHETTI

Here is a fancied-up version of spaghetti that you can also freeze into individual servings. Wonderful on a cold evening!

1-2 pkgs. spaghetti (or any pasta that you prefer)
1 jar prepared spaghetti sauce
1 lb. ground round (no more than 15 percent fat), ground turkey or ground sausage (mild)
1 small onion, chopped
2 tbsp. crushed garlic (Note: I prefer the kind in a jar that you can find in your grocery's deli case or produce department.)
2 tsp. Italian seasoning
1 cup each mozzarella and mild cheddar cheese, grated

Preheat oven to 350° F. Prepare spaghetti according to package instructions in a large pot; drain and return to pot. Brown meat in large saucepan and drain, return to saucepan. Add entire jar of sauce, onion, garlic and Italian seasoning to meat, stirring thoroughly. Add sauce mixture to spaghetti pot and mix thoroughly. Pour contents into a casserole and layer top with cheese. Bake at 350° until cheese is completely melted.

**GOES GREAT WITH:** A romaine and butter lettuce salad topped with Italian dressing and crusty garlic bread or garlic rolls.

## ALMOND CHICKEN

So quick and easy! I found this recipe years ago and will be eternally grateful to its creator!

**½ cup finely chopped almonds**
**¼ cup brown sugar**
**½ tsp. garlic powder**
**4 boneless, skinless chicken breasts**

Preheat oven to 400° F. Combine almonds, brown sugar and garlic powder in a bowl. Dredge chicken in the almond-brown sugar mixture. Place chicken on a baking sheet covered with aluminum foil. Pat remaining mixture on top of each piece of chicken. Bake for eighteen to twenty minutes or until an instant-read meat thermometer (which I could NOT live without) registers 160°.

**GOES GREAT WITH:** Baked potato and sautéed green beans with crumbled bacon or real bacon bits.

## CAROLE'S BEST-EVER ROAST CHICKEN

This recipe takes a little longer to prepare, but it is *so* worth it. I created this recipe many years ago for a High Holy Days dinner at home, but it's just too good to have only once a year! You'll need a roasting rack and your trusty instant-read meat thermometer.

**One 5 to 8 lb. roasting chicken, cleaned and trimmed of fat**
**Pepper**
**Crushed garlic (fresh or from a jar)**
**1 cup prepared yellow mustard**
**¾ cup brown sugar**
**1 small can crushed pineapple, drained**

Preheat oven to 350° F. Combine mustard, brown sugar and crushed pineapple in bowl, set aside. Season chicken with pepper and garlic to preference and place breast side down on roasting rack on a baking sheet covered with heavy-duty aluminum foil. Place chicken in oven. After thirty minutes, turn baking sheet around for even baking. After one hour, take an instant-read temperature and then baste chicken with mustard mixture.

Check chicken every thirty minutes and continue to baste with mustard mixture as preferred until instant-read thermometer reads 160° when inserted at the thickest part of the chicken. Remove and let stand for fifteen minutes prior to carving.

**GOES GREAT WITH:** Additional mustard sauce for "dipping", mashed potatoes and sautéed spinach with pine nuts (pignolis).

## FRUITY FLUFF

Need a dessert in a hurry? This one is not only healthy and low in calories, it's also so easy to put together that I feel like I should apologize for the fact that it isn't more complicated. Then again, do you really *need* anything that's complicated?

**1 lb. (16 oz.) container cottage cheese**
**1 pkg. (3 oz.) fruit-flavored gelatin (orange is a flavor of choice)**
**1 can (20 oz.) crushed pineapple, drained**
**1 12 oz container "lite" whipped topping (such as Cool Whip), thawed**

Mix all ingredients together. Chill for approximately one hour before serving. Refrigerate leftovers.

## LET'S "MOVE IT"

Since it may be all you can do to get out of bed on some days, the very thought of "exercise" (as in running to the gym or jumping up and down in front of the DVD player) can be exhausting. Believe me, I know. I also know that you will do wonders for your own well-being if you take just a few minutes to "clear the cobwebs" and move just a little bit.

The easiest way to do this is to simply go for a walk. Not "power walk" in fancy stretch pants with three-pound weights and headphones; there will be time for that later. Just go outside your house or apartment and walk around your neighborhood. If it's cold, bundle up. If it's hot, wait until sunset when it's cooler. Take deep breaths. Enjoy the twilight of evening or the breaking of morning. Even if your walk lasts just ten minutes, you will return relaxed and refreshed.

---

## FROM THE STILETTO FILE

Safety Girl again with a couple of reminders:

1. Never leave your home without **carrying some kind of identification**. It also doesn't hurt to **carry your cell phone** with you.
2. **Be aware of your surroundings at all times**. Walk in safe, well-lit and populated areas.
3. **Wear light-colored clothing** and **walk on a sidewalk** wherever possible.

---

## EXERCISE EXCUSES ERASED!

The number one excuse that women give for not exercising is lack of time. I know this, because it's certainly MY number one excuse. What if I were to give you a few sure-fire exercises that will help tone you up and make you feel great—that not only take about ten minutes in the morning (and/or ten minutes at night if you wish) but will also give you great results?

I thought that might get your attention!

The following exercises are easy, effective, FAST and will help you strengthen and tone your arms, upper back, lower abs, rear and thighs. Even if you don't think that you need "exercise", you'll wind up feeling better and that is our ultimate goal.

As with any new exercise program, you need to consider any physical limitations that you may have and you should consult with your physician prior to beginning. Read on for Carole's Terrific Tone-Up Plan.

Photos courtesy of Carole Brody Fleet

## "DOC CRUNCH"

Like most caregivers, my back had suffered as a result of caring for my husband during his illness. This exercise was originally recommended to me by an orthopedic surgeon to help strengthen my lower back. Guess what—not only did my back benefit, but so did my abs!

This crunch is slightly different than the more conventional crunch. The move is far more isolated, which really works the lower abdomen, one of the most difficult areas to tone. Lie on the floor, knees bent, feet flat on the floor with your hands behind your head. Now lift your head slightly while pulling the small of your back to the floor—almost like you're trying to pull your belly button in toward your spine. Executed correctly, it only takes a very small amount of lifting—you won't wind up with an aching neck. Start out slowly, do as many crunches as you can, working up to high numbers as your strength increases.

Photos courtesy of Carole Brody Fleet

### "BOOTY PUSH"

This fantastic move comes to you courtesy of my daughter, resident cheerleader and athletic expert. It's an awesome way to tone thighs and rear (and once again, you'll find that your abs will benefit as well). This exercise looks a little peculiar, but who cares...it works!

Lie on the floor, knees bent, feet flat, hands by your sides. Push your pelvis toward the ceiling until your lower body is at a 45 degree angle (take care not to overextend or arch your back). As you push up, squeeze your butt and release as you lower to original position. As with the Doc Crunch, start out slow and work up to higher numbers as you become stronger.

## THE WONDER OF WEIGHTS

I don't know of anyone who couldn't benefit from mild weight training. Coincidentally, I also don't know of one woman who does not complain about the condition of her arms and/or her upper back! The good news is that these are two of the easiest (and fastest!) areas to tone on the entire body.

You'll need either 3 pound or 5 pound hand weights for these exercises. Do (or work up to) three sets of twelve reps per set at least three times per week.

### BICEP CURLS

This is as basic as it gets, ladies! Stand with your feet shoulder width apart, knees slightly bent, arms down in front of your thighs, fists facing up grasping weights. Curl arms inward up to shoulder, stopping short of touching the shoulder.

### THE BUTTERFLY

This is a great move for the shoulders and outer arms. Stand with your feet shoulder width apart, knees slightly bent, arms bent at waist-level, fists facing toward one another grasping weights. Keeping arms bent, lift arms up until they are even with shoulders and fists face down. Do not lift arms higher than shoulder level. Return to original start position.

### THE BACKSCRATCHER

You know that "chicken neck" underarm that we all either dread or already are complaining about? This exercise will take care of that potential "waddle" under the arm. Stand with your feet shoulder-width apart, knees slightly bent, arms grasping weights straight overhead. Slowly lower weights straight down behind you, taking care not to arch your back. Return to original position.

## FROM CAROLE'S JUKEBOX

There is very little that I do without music involved and exercise is certainly no exception. You don't have to move "in time" to the music, but your energy level will automatically increase when you put on your favorite feel-good tunes. Here are just a very few of my absolute can't-sit-still-to-it favorites:

1. "Let's Get It Started", Black Eyed Peas
2. "Walk Away", Kelly Clarkson
3. "SexyBack", Justin Timberlake
4. "Black Horse and the Cherry Tree", K.T. Tunstall
5. "Baby I'm a Star" and "Let's Get Crazy", Prince
6. "Bust a Move", Young MC
7. "One Thing Leads to Another", The Fixx
8. "Let's Get Loud", Jennifer Lopez
9. "Rewind", Natasha Slayton
10. "Ain't No Other Man", Christina Aguilera
11. "You Spin Me Right Round", Dead or Alive
12. "Now That We've Found Love", Heavy D & The Boyz
13. "Unbelievable", EMF
14. "Objection", Shakira
15. "Cha Cha Slide", Mr. C
16. "Groove is in the Heart", Deee-Lite

## JUST FOR YOU

By now you may be thinking, "Okay Carole, let me get this straight. I'm supposed to work, have grief time, worry about my clothes, hair, makeup, meal preparation, exercising—that sounds so selfish; it's not all about me and besides, there aren't enough hours in the day."

Well if it's not all about you, then who IS it all about? Yes, it is all about you!

If you're a parent, I know that "the child(ren) come first." I'm a parent too and I have the same tendency that you do: to put myself third or fifth or eighth behind all of the child's needs and activities and the to-do lists. If you're not a parent, you may still feel like taking care of yourself is pointless or a waste of time—or you just don't feel like you want to make any effort. However, all of the suggestions and activities that we are talking about truly are not "selfish" or overly time consuming. The bottom line is—pay attention please:

---

### You have time for that which you *choose* to have time.

---

*Choose* to have time for **YOU**. *Choose* to pay attention to your health—physical and emotional. *Choose* to pay attention to your appearance once again. You will be healthier, happier and more productive at work and if you are a parent, you are going to be a far better parent to those little faces that you love so much when you take care of YOU! Most importantly, you will be better suited to face the tasks at hand each day *and* progress on your healing journey when you take these positive measures to be healthy in mind, body and spirit. At the risk of sounding like a well-known commercial, don't you believe that you're worth it? I KNOW for a fact that you are!

## YOUR PERSONAL "GETTING BETTER EVERY DAY" GOAL SHEET

Virtually every mentor, teacher, coach (myself included!), athlete and success story both teaches and lives by one very common statement: "A dream is just that, until you write it down…then it becomes a goal."

The same applies here. It's one thing to *want* to feel better and to think about feeling better and to be "sick and tired of being sick and tired", but it's quite another thing to actually *do* something about it. So let's quit dreaming and start "doing" by seeing where we can make some adjustments and set some goals for your healthy renewal of body and spirit.

### WATCH OUT "GIRL IN THE MIRROR"…HERE I COME!

Mark the answer that best describes you:

**1. My standard "Don't Look At Me/I Don't Care About Anything/Hiding Out From the World" Outfit consists of:**

• Torn flannel pajamas.
• Baggy sweats.
• Anything that is oversized, overworn and "under-flattering".

### MY PROMISE TO ME

Right after I get rid of my "Don't Look At Me/I Don't Care About Anything/Hiding Out From the World" Outfit, I am no longer going to make excuses for not putting on clothes that I love and in which I feel great. The one single change that I promise to make in order to get out of my "fashion rut" is:

_____

_____

**2. My idea of pampering is:**

• A half-day at a spa, a massage, a manicure/pedicure…or all three.
• Enjoying a fabulous meal that I don't have to cook or clean up after.
• Reading the Bible, a grief book or other meditative volume.
• What's pampering?

## MY PROMISE TO ME

Realizing that I have earned the right to enjoy whatever my idea of pampering is, the one pampering activity that I promise to myself is:

_____

_____

    I promise to do this for myself beginning on _____ and will do this for myself at least _____ times a week.

    (Please note: "when I get around to it" is not a day of the week! Commit to a start date as well as how many times you will "treat" yourself per week.)

### 3. At bedtime, I:

- Need to take something medicinal; otherwise, forget about sleep.
- Pay bills, watch television or otherwise engage in a distracting activity—or five.
- Wind up staying up most of the night—I think I may never sleep again.
- Sleep is not problematic for me (skip to Question 4).

## MY PROMISE TO ME

I understand that sleep is an essential part of the renewal of my health. In order to achieve restful sleep, starting **tonight** I am going to try the following ideas from this chapter. I also understand that if sleep continues to be a problem, I am **not** going to simply ignore it. I am going to consult with my doctor if this problem persists.

_____

_____

### 4. Overall, my (or our, if you have children) meals consist of:

- Fast-food (more than three times a week).
- Mostly home-prepared meals (and no, frozen dinners don't count!).
- Grab-and-go (a sandwich; coffee and a doughnut, etc.).

## MY PROMISE TO ME

Even though I may not have much of an appetite right now, I understand that healthy eating is an essential part of my recovery. I will do my utmost to limit fast-food and/or processed foods to no more than twice a week. I am going to try some eating suggestions and recipes, either from this chapter, from the Recommended Reading or from my own recipe files:

_____

_____

**5. My exercise habits consist of:**

- A regular daily workout.
- Housecleaning, grocery shopping, running kids to school and their activities.
- Watching exercise infomercials or my child's sports practices.

## MY PROMISE TO ME

I understand that moving even just a little bit is going to help me feel better emotionally and mentally. I am going to try some of the suggestions, either from this chapter or from other resources that I have found:

_____

_____

I promise to do this for myself beginning on _____ and will do this for myself at least _____ times a week.

(Please note: "Someday" isn't a day of the week either. Write a start date down, how many times a week you are going to "move" and commit to it!)

You'll feel better. I promise.

### Chapter 7

# THE "BUSINESS" OF WIDOWHOOD

### (Or: The "Wherefores" and "What Nows" of Paperwork)

As important as healing your mind and your heart are, practical matters must sometimes take precedence over the emotional. Despite your overwhelming grief, whether we like it or not, life does have a way of intruding. Children still need care, the household needs to continue operating and creditors and banks, while sympathetic, still want their payments on time and in full. Though the practical is likely the very last thing you want to be concerned with, and immediately after the funeral would be one of the worst times to have to worry about anything (let alone the drudgery of financial matters), procrastination is unfortunately not an option.

In and of itself, the practical can be overwhelming. Moreover, I happen to be one of those types who get overwhelmed easily and will throw everything into the air, walk away and ultimately accomplish nothing. However, I found that when I took ONE task at a time, one DAY at a time, everything eventually got done in a timely and organized fashion.

Because the practical is not only unavoidable, it must be addressed as quickly as possible. We begin with…

## The Paper Trail

I know what you're thinking.

Yuck.

I, too, would rather watch paint dry than have to search for, shuffle, organize, re-organize, sort through and collate PAPER. Yet it's a necessary and time-urgent part of the process. Look at it this way: the sooner we get your paperwork in order, parties notified and income generated, the sooner we can get back to the really important matters—like YOU!

The most important key here is organization, especially for the purpose of follow up. You absolutely will not be able to recall telephone conversations, keep dates "in your head" or have letters and papers scattered every which way. With everything that you've had to deal with up to this point, you are "scattered" enough right now. A very simple "system", where everything is kept in one place and in order, will not only keep you organized and thinking much more clearly, you will also feel far less overwhelmed by the "business" aspect of widowhood.

---

### LET'S GET ORGANIZED

Before you begin to make your telephone calls and subsequently begin amassing promised dates of claims completion, letters of confirmation, documentation checklists, etc., you will need to have:

- A legal pad.
- A three-inch, three-ring binder with a "pocket" on the inside left cover.
- A three-hole punch.
- Alpha dividers. You will be filing notes of telephone conversations, what each entity requests, etc., alphabetically by entity or company name.
- A business-style diary or At-A-Glance calendar for the purposes of calendaring follow-up dates.

---

As you begin to receive confirmation letters, letters of instruction, insurance payouts and similar things, you can clip everything alphabetically in one place. The pocket in the front of the binder is a good place to keep all of the original personal paperwork that you have gathered on your own.

You will need a calendar that is separate from your regular family date book, so that you will be able to note follow-up dates clearly and accurately. For example, if an agent tells you to expect an insurance claim payout within "ten business days", you will need a ready calendar so that if the check doesn't arrive within the promised time, you will then be able to call and inquire as to the status. The other important reason for keeping this calendar separate from the family activity calendar is so that an important follow-up call or letter date doesn't inadvertently get missed or mixed up with a notation about your child's activities.

I prefer a month-at-a-glance calendar, so that I can see all thirty days in front of me, easily count off "business days" (very important, so that you don't inadvertently count a holiday or weekend as a business day) and have a separate section for notes within the month. These items will not only keep you organized and keep things from getting lost, you'll also stay on track and on top of all of the dates on which to expect actions that you are promised.

So, as the song says, let's start at the very beginning.

## YOUR LIST OF "MUST- HAVES"

You will need to have the following paperwork and items readily at hand:

- Original (if in your possession) and/or a copy of your husband's last will and testament.
- His Social Security card (or number). If you don't know his number nor have it handy, his medical records will contain that information.
- Driver's license (both yours and his) or other government-issued identification.
- Checkbooks, passbooks and records of all financial accounts and holdings, such as mutual fund statements, CD's, IRA's, 401(k)'s, etc. This means *all accounts*, whether they are held jointly by the two of you or individually by your husband. You don't need every single bank statement; just the most recent. Depending upon the type of account and the financial institution, this information may be found online as well.
- Life insurance policies (the declarations page will usually be sufficient).
- Marriage certificate.
- Any paperwork pertaining to military service (such as a DD-214).
- Original death certificate(s) when received.

These items should be kept together; preferably in the front pocket of your three-ring binder. If there is too much paperwork, create a separate file in a manila folder and keep the folder inside the binder.

The most time-urgent things that need to be done include anything that involves generating income for you and your family quickly, so that if at all possible, bill-paying is not interrupted. Each company will inform you of what claims they will need to file on your behalf and remove names from accounts. Use your legal pad to make a list of what each requires, using separate sheets of paper for each. You don't want any delays, because someone didn't get the right piece of paper or because you lost a phone number that was written on a "sticky note".

It is of the utmost importance that you *always* write down with whom you spoke, the date and time that you spoke with the person and a quick note as to the content of the conversation. You can then clip the note(s) into your binder, so that the name of the person with whom you are working as well as the substance of your conversation(s) will be readily on hand. Don't forget to place the follow-up date on your calendar!

## TELEPHONE TIME

You will want to call these entities in the suggested priority immediately:

- Social Security office.
- Veterans Administration (if your husband was in the armed forces at any time during his life. His status with the military at the time of his death does not matter).
- The human resources department of your husband's place of employment (for life insurance claims and continuation of medical insurance if you are medically insured through his employer).
- Life insurance companies (if there exists separate policies apart from his employer).
- Bank/Mortgagor (especially important if they hold a credit life insurance policy on your home. Credit life insurance is defined in this chapter. Your bank will also advise you as to what you'll need to change the title on your home).

After the "income generation" calling is complete, you should then continue with:

- Credit card companies.
- Department of Motor Vehicles (to transfer title of any automobiles, boats or other vehicles on which your husband is a registered owner).
- Accountant or whomever you retain to do your tax returns.
- Post office.

## JUST FOR YOU

After the phone calling/list making is done, SO ARE YOU. Put the paperwork away for the day and take a well-deserved break. If at all possible, this would be an excellent point to enjoy your Quiet Time for the day.

Once you have completed telephoning the people and organizations necessary, it's a bit of a waiting game, as, generally speaking, no action(s) will be taken absent a death certificate. This includes life insurance payouts, credit life insurance payouts, government benefits paid and title changes effected. Depending on where you live, receipt of the death certificates can take anywhere from ten days to a month or more from the date of death. This is usually a task that your funeral director or hospice director can take care of on your behalf and typically costs only the amount of the certificate itself.

---

### FROM THE STILETTO FILE

The cost and time parameters for obtaining death certificates differ from state to state as well as county to county within your state. Your funeral director will have that information. At her recommendation, I had our director order twelve certificates, so that any entity requesting an "original" certificate would have one and that I would have at least one for my records as well. Entities such as credit card companies will usually be satisfied with a photocopy of the certificate.

Once ordered, the death certificates are generally mailed directly to you. Be sure to calendar a follow-up with whomever you charged with ordering the certificates, so that you will have an approximate idea of when you can expect them to be delivered. If you do not receive them within the reasonably expected time frame, contact the person who ordered the certificates to re-confirm the order date, the time parameter for delivery and further instructions for follow-up. This is a vital step, because everyone with whom you have made contact is waiting for this single piece of paper before any further actions are taken.

## CRY AND CARRY ON

The day that the certificates arrive is a sad day indeed—it's a "confirmation" in black-and-white that your spouse's death and all it entails is really happening and it's really happening to you. It's important that you carefully review the certificates for accuracy (correct spelling of all names, dates, times, circumstances surrounding death, attending physician if any and other pertinent information) then put them aside, make yourself a cup of tea (chamomile is my tea of choice) and allow yourself to be sad. IT IS OKAY!

### Follow Up and Follow Through

You MUST be prepared to follow up and follow through with all of the entities with whom you need to be in contact: filing claims, switching accounts, credit cards, etc. In the idyllic place called Perfect World, everyone would be doing his or her job to the best of the person's ability and everything would be done on time and with seamless efficiency. However, we live in the Real World and we know that things don't always happen "as promised and on time."

When it comes to governmental agencies, credit card companies and most major banks, you are one of thousands of people with whom they are dealing every single day. Paperwork sometimes gets lost or mislaid, personnel get sick, transferred or fired; in other words, "stuff happens." Be aware that it is going to be entirely up to you to stay in contact until the task is completed—your "job" is to make sure that everyone is doing their jobs.

Once you have received the death certificates, you can then get to work by sending each company or entity what they have requested. Remember, take ONE matter at a time—even one a DAY is fine! The following is a recommended order in which you should work.

### a. Social Security

Although the government's reputation is usually one of bureaucracy, red tape and run-around, I personally found the employees at Social Security to be quite sympathetic to my situation and very easy to work with. The Social Security official website at **www.ssa.gov** is an excellent place to visit prior to contacting Social Security and filing your claim. Although you will not be able to apply online for widows' benefits, surviving children's benefits or the one-time lump sum death benefit, you will find extremely valuable information, including:

1. The toll-free telephone number(s) that you will need to initiate contact.

2. A ZIP code locator that will allow you to find the Social Security office nearest to your home. This is necessary for the delivery of requested documents.

3. A thorough explanation of who qualifies for Social Security benefits for survivors.

4. A complete list of questions that you will be asked upon contacting Social Security. Reviewing this list prior to contact will allow you to be prepared in advance, should you need documentation to provide answers either over the telephone or in person.

Do not delay the filing of a Social Security claim if you do not have all of the documentation that they request—if necessary, Social Security will assist you in obtaining the needed documents. You must have your husband's Social Security number; however, you do not need to have his original card if it is not available to you.

If you have minor children, you need to file on their behalves for separate survivor benefits. If some of your children are stepchildren to your late husband (as was the case with me), Social Security will make a determination of his financial responsibilities to your children by percentage and their survivor benefits will be based upon that figure. Adopted children are considered as if they were naturally-born children. When determining your eligibility for survivor benefits, your age, as well as your personal income will be taken into consideration.

Social Security will ask you for certain documents and, unlike most other entities (credit card companies, banks, etc.), they will need *original* documents. Don't worry, you will be provided with a list of what they want to see in support of your claim. My suggestion is to, if at all possible, deliver these documents *in person* to your local Social Security office and ask to be notified as to when you can pick them up. You will then be notified by mail as to what your benefits will be and when they will begin as well as whether or not you have qualified for the one-time Social Security death benefit.

---

### FROM THE STILETTO FILE

Although it is certainly permitted, contrary to popular belief **you do not require a lawyer** to file your claim on your behalf or for your children with Social Security. Unless you feel that you have been wrongly denied benefits and need to go through an appeals process, do not retain legal counsel for initial filing of survivor benefits. Social Security employees will assist you to the best of their abilities—save your money!

---

### b. Veterans Administration

If your husband died while on active duty with the armed forces or if he is a veteran of the armed forces, you will want to contact the Veterans Administration to see if you qualify for numerous survivor benefits, including pensions, benefits on behalf of minor children, medical benefits, home loans, student loans, etc. The Veterans Administration website at **www.va.gov** will be an incredible source of information for you and is self-explanatory in getting you to the areas of the site that you will specifically need to initiate a claim. For example, the claims forms required for someone who died while on active military duty will be different than those claims forms required for someone who was a veteran.

In addition, the site has links to other federal agencies and organizations that offer related services that you may need, including bereavement counseling. The site also has downloadable forms and you will be thoroughly instructed as to which forms you will need, based on your late husband's military status at the time of his death and the specific benefits that you are seeking.

### c. Place of Employment

Contact your husband's place of employment and speak with the Human Resources Department, office manager or to whoever handles the insurance claims with his company. Generally, they will file the life insurance claim on your behalf and let you know what documents the insurance company will need from you. The same goes for any continuing benefits to which you may be personally entitled, such as medical and life insurance. Unless otherwise directed to do so, do not contact the insurance companies directly; let those in the position to assist you do so. For example, since my husband was a retired police officer, the POA (Police Officers' Association) helped me with all of the requisite paperwork needed to continue medical insurance for my daughter and myself; I made one telephone call and they did the rest (for which I will be forever grateful!).

If your husband was on state disability, private sector disability, unemployment or any other government or private assistance at the time of his death, you will need to contact the appropriate agency IMMEDIATELY—you don't want them to continue paying benefits and then discover overpayment after the fact!

### d. Life Insurance

Your husband may have separate life policies outside of his employment. For example, many people carry "burial policies" or insurance specifically designed to cover basic funeral expenses. He may have had a separate term life insurance policy outside of his employer. If your husband had any life insurance policies apart from a policy provided at or through his employment, contact the holding insurance companies immediately. They will make a note on the account and advise you as to what they will require to process your claim.

Happily, once the appropriate paperwork has been received, life insurance policies pay fairly quickly. In addition to the life insurance payout, they will generally refund any overpayment of premium in that claim payout. For instance, if the death occurs in mid-December and the policy premium was paid through March 31 of the following year, in addition to the insurance payout, the insurance company will refund overpayment of the premium from the date that the death occurred in December through March 31.

### e. Bank/Mortgage Company

Notify your bank and ask what is required to have checking and savings accounts, Certificates of Deposit and any other type(s) of accounts transferred into your name solely. If the accounts are held jointly, this will be an easy process. If your husband held accounts in his name alone, the bank will have specific instructions for you and may need to see your husband's will, along with other documentation.

The same will apply for the mortgage on your home. Some mortgage companies will ask that you file a Notice of Death of Joint Tenant (or a similar form) in order to reissue the title on your home to your name alone. Again, this requirement will vary from state to state and many counties provide the appropriate form(s) on the Internet, along with instructions for filing with your local court.

While the re-issuance of the title or grant deed in your name does not technically involve income generation at the outset, should you wish to refinance or sell your home at a later date, the transaction will be complicated if your deceased husband's name remains on the title. You'll avoid a whole lot of paperwork entanglements and delays in completion of financial transactions involving your home if you can complete this as soon as is feasible. Again, you do not need a lawyer for this purpose.

Additionally, if you hold "credit life insurance" on your house and the policy is not held by your bank or mortgage company, you will want to contact the holding insurance company immediately. Depending on how the policy was written, you may be entitled to partial or full benefits to either reduce the balance on your mortgage or pay off your mortgage in full.

### f. Credit card companies

Not unlike Social Security, credit card companies have also earned a bit of a "reputation" that precedes them; what with skyrocketing interest rates, seemingly endless voicemail systems and late fees that occur at 12:01 a.m., literally one minute after your payment due date. In spite of this reputation, I am thrilled to reassure you that without exception, every single credit card company with whom I dealt was wonderfully understanding and extremely helpful—one major credit card company even sent a note of sympathy to me.

Each company has different requirements as to what they needed to either close or change the accounts. For example, one company didn't want a death certificate; rather, they asked for a program from the funeral. Some accounts will need to be "closed and re-opened" in your name alone; others will simply remove your husband's name.

Virtually every major credit card company offers "credit life insurance". Like the credit life insurance that you may have on your home, this means that for a premium usually included on the monthly bill, if something happens to the credit card holder, the credit life insurance will immediately pay off any remaining balances on the card that were left at the time of death. If you are unsure as to whether credit life insurance exists on the accounts, be sure to check with each credit card company prior to sending any additional funds. If this coverage exists, the credit life insurance will immediately pay off any remaining balances. They will ask for documentation that substantiates the death and this documentation will differ from company to company. They will note your account and in some cases, they may hold the account in abeyance and not require any payment until they receive the requested documentation.

---

### FROM THE STILETTO FILE

You may not be responsible for debts that were accrued in your husband's name alone either during or prior to your marriage. If accounts exist for which you are not financially responsible (you aren't an authorized user on a credit card, he has a bank line of credit in his name alone, he acquired the debt prior to your marriage, etc.), contact your local Lawyer Referral Service and find out if you are responsible for these debts. However, if you are an "authorized user" on a credit card, you will be responsible for any outstanding balances.

---

### g. Department of Motor Vehicles

You will need to consult with your state's Department of Motor Vehicles in order to determine what paperwork will be necessary to remove your husband's name from the title on your automobile(s) as well as any other vehicles or boats that you may own. Though it may not seem important or as though it would matter whether or not your late husband's name is on the titles to your vehicles, please bear in mind that all registered owners of vehicles involved in an accident may be held liable. In other words, if you are involved in an accident that results in a lawsuit and your husband's name is still on the title of the vehicle, your husband could be named as a defendant. Once a suing party (the plaintiff) determines that your husband is deceased, they could potentially sue your husband's estate.

Most forms requiring such changes are available online and it is not a complicated process. Contact your local Department of Motor Vehicles for further information.

### h. Accountant

This one is quick and easy, two words that I love. Let your accountant know of your situation and be aware that come tax season, you may be eligible to file under what is referred to as "Preferred Status" with the

Internal Revenue Service. This means that your status as a widow will be noted on the return; however, the return will be considered as if you were married, thereby affording you the same tax benefits as if you were married. Your accountant will be able to provide you with additional information.

**i. Post office**
Notify the post office that your husband is deceased—they will make a note of this data with your address and it will remain on file for a year.

## CRY AND CARRY ON

Notifying the post office will not completely eliminate the delivery of mail to your husband, especially junk mail and advertising. Seeing Mike's name on letters in the mailbox every day did nothing for the healing process. In fact, for a good six months after Mike's death, I kept receiving advertising for *grave markers and headstones!*

After wishing these "junk pushers" flat tires on the freeway in the middle of rush hour and after having tried to ignore the continued onslaught of junk and subsequently discovering that this tactic doesn't work either, I began writing "Deceased, Return to Sender" in red marker and mailing *all* of the junk, advertising, unsolicited magazines and catalogs, etc., back to the respective senders. Since these companies have to pay for that mail to get returned, they eventually quit sending it.

## Where There's a Will...

Hopefully, your husband had some kind of will, formal or informal, that will direct the disposition of real and liquid assets as well as his personal property. Make sure that you have the will in your possession (the original and at least two copies). If your husband did not have a will at the time of his death and entities such as banks or insurance companies are slow to act absent a will, you may wish to contact your local Lawyer Referral Service to speak with someone who specializes in estate matters.

Please be aware that the handling of wills and probate are different in each state—for example, I did not have to probate Mike's will in the state of California (where we resided), but for matters concerning the sale of property that we jointly owned in the state of Texas, his will needed to go through the probate process in Texas.

## JUST FOR YOU

Wills are not just for the "rich and famous" or for those with large estates and vast holdings. If you own so much as a car and/or you have any kind of life insurance policy (even if it's a small policy held through your employer), you need a will—period.

Make sure that you have a will in order—it can even be handwritten, but regardless of the size of your estate, make sure that you HAVE ONE! Also make sure that you have all of your important papers in one easy-to-find location so your loved ones do not need to go on a scavenger hunt. This is possibly the greatest gift that you can leave behind—the gift of organization!

### For the Not-So-New Young Widow

If you've been widowed for some time and, while reading these different steps, you've come upon something that you forgot—perhaps a claim that you didn't file or a benefit to which you didn't realize you might be entitled, don't simply assume that "it's too late" or that "too much time has passed." Contact whomever it is that you either forgot to contact or whom you didn't realize you should have contacted and request immediate assistance. Some widows do not realize to what benefits they may be entitled, so don't draw conclusions without all of the facts first.

## JUST FOR YOU

### Easy Does It

Remember, while all of these things must be done as soon as possible, they all don't have to be done all at once in the same day—IT WILL ALL GET DONE. When you start to feel tired, overwhelmed, irritated or are just plain "over it" for the day, put it down and walk away.

## CAROLE'S KEEP-YOU-TOGETHER CHECKLIST

<u>Clip this page on the front of your binder
on top of the alpha dividers.</u>

- I have contacted all entities that have anything to do with the immediate generation of income to my household (Social Security, Veterans Administration, husband's employer, life insurance companies, etc.) as listed in this chapter.

- I have contacted the person(s) in charge of obtaining the death certificates. They were ordered on _____ and should arrive on or before _____. I have calendared to follow up on _____.

- I have contacted my bank and/or mortgage company, all credit card companies, the Department of Motor Vehicles, my accountant and the post office to make all necessary account and title changes.

- I have gathered all paperwork that each entity has requested as listed in this chapter and I have calendared to follow up with each entity to make sure that everyone is doing what they have promised to do by or before the date promised to me.

- I have a basic will of my own; it and other important papers are in order and in an easy-to-find location. At least two people know where to find this information.

### Chapter 8

# WHEN BOTH MOMMY AND DADDY...ARE YOU

## (...Or So You Think)

In addition to your own anguish and the transition into a new life that you are making, you are also charged with a tremendous responsibility: that of helping your children move forward into a life without Daddy. This includes aiding them in working through their grief and reinforcing security and stability within the house and in their day-to-day living. One of the central aspects that differentiates the young widow from the traditional widow demographic is the fact that a great majority of young widows have young and/or adolescent children.

Instructing mothers on how best to "parent", especially during this time filled with sorrow and heartache, is very difficult. The simple fact is that absolutely no one knows your child better than you. I also acknowledge that you may disagree with some of the suggestions, opinions and insights I'm going to offer. However, I believe we can all benefit from the different perspectives of others, especially when it comes to the welfare of our children. This chapter features tried-and-true suggestions and solutions, including some that I successfully utilized with my own child during our early grieving process, that I hope may enable you to better aid and support your children through this, one of the most difficult periods that they will ever endure.

There is no "right" or "wrong" way to do things here—just some ideas and suggestions that are offered with love and encouragement. Though some of the suggestions may be somewhat "controversial" and not all will agree, please consider these insights carefully, while keeping the ages and genders of your children in mind as to suitability. You may also wish to discuss this with your family physician, your child's pediatrician or a counselor.

## The Agony...and the End

As was the case with my daughter, if children are dealing with the death of their father after a long illness, they will naturally grieve; however, they will also likely feel a certain measure of relief (as may you!) that the illness and his suffering has come to an end. This is perfectly normal, since watching your loved one "die by inches" is about as painful as it gets.

Do not be offended if your children express these feelings of relief that the illness has come to an end, even though the end of the illness also meant the end of their father's life. Additionally, should your children experience feelings of guilt, because they feel relieved that "it's finally over", please hasten to reassure them that you realize that the children were not "wishing" their father's death; they were simply wishing an end to everyone's pain—especially that of the children's father.

Even with this "relief", after you have allayed feelings of guilt, your children will still go through the same feelings of shock at the **reality** of the death. Remember, until this moment, death was "conceptual": as long as death was still a concept, somewhere in the back of their minds there was still a grain of hope that their dad was going to get better. There might have even been outright denial that the death was going to occur at all. Now, their father's death has also become their sad reality.

## "But He Was Just Here..."

Conversely, if your husband's passing was sudden, there will be much shock, disbelief and anger, regardless of the circumstances surrounding the sudden death, be it illness (such as a heart attack or stroke), accident or a tragedy. In many respects, this is an even more difficult death to assimilate for a child because he was playing ball with Dad just yesterday or she just had a nice breakfast with Dad this morning. Without warning, without provocation, for no good reason, Dad is gone.

Your child may likely first express feelings of anger and unfortunately, this anger may very well be channeled toward you. As human beings and certainly as children, though they do not mean to, they tend to strike out at the ones whom they love the most. This is because deep down in our children's hearts they know they can. They know they can be angry, mean, loud and horrid and that when all is said and done, Mom is going to love them anyway.

Let's now examine other helpful means of coping for (and with) your children as they begin their own healing journeys.

## The Funeral—and the Following Day

Most funerals are followed by some sort of "reception" or fellowship period, where mourners have the opportunity to pay respects to the family of the deceased. There are usually trays of food and in some circles, occasionally even music. For example, in Judaism we "sit Shiva", where, along with at-home prayer services, this kind of "fellowship" goes on for the seven days following the funeral (minus the music).

Whether immediately after the funeral or at subsequent gatherings in memory of your husband for the period following the funeral, you might be shocked to see your young children running around playing happily with one another or your older children socializing and laughing as though they were at a Friday night football game. This is not in any way disrespectful to the memory of their father or a dishonor to you. This is, in a fashion, a coping mechanism.

Younger children see food being served, their family and friends naturally behaving in ways conducive to a "party atmosphere". Understand that they are still acutely aware of the circumstances and in their own ways are trying to cope by distracting themselves. As long as they behave in a manner befitting the surroundings (in other words, running around screaming and yelling is not appropriate in a church or synagogue social hall or in a funeral home), allow them their freedom to relax and make themselves comfortable.

Older children obviously are more attuned as to what exactly is going on and they are truly caught "betwixt and between". They still are children dealing with the loss of their father; yet they may feel like they have to assume "adult" roles—and they have almost assuredly been told at least once by someone that they have to "be strong" for you (yes, some people say dumb things to children as well).

Your older children will naturally want to spend time with anyone in their age groups in attendance and the conversations will drift to normal adolescent discussion; be it about school, a social activity, who won the ball game or who is in love with whom this week. They also know that there will be time enough to "dwell" on the tragic circumstances that have befallen all of you. Allow them then this opportunity to relax. Understanding that decorum and discretion are the orders of the day, permit them to be enveloped and comforted by others as they best see fit.

The age of your children notwithstanding, an overall feeling of surrealism surrounds this funeral period—as though all of this is happening to someone else. Reality will hit them soon enough.

## JUST FOR YOU

The day after the funeral may likely be even more difficult than the funeral itself. The day of the funeral is filled with activity, bustle and people; all very distracting factors. As I outlined in the introduction, the day after the funeral everyone has "gone home" and gone on with their lives, leaving you and your children alone with your collective heartache. My strongest recommendation for the day following the funeral is do absolutely nothing. Nothing. No household chores, no errand-running—this even includes the "business" of widowhood; that too can wait just one more day. Take this day to sleep in, drink tea, sit and stare into space, cuddle together, take a deep breath and absorb the enormity of what has happened to all of you.

Though this may again be a controversial suggestion, I do not recommend that children return to school the day immediately following the funeral. I promise that your children's eventual academic performances or college admissions will not hinge on the day or few days of school that they may miss. Make sure that your children's teachers are advised as to the family's current circumstances, so that they can support your children in turn. Anyone who has offered assistance to you will be happy to obtain make-up work from school. Older children will be able to get help from friends in the same classes. Give your children the opportunity to "catch their breaths" as well; let them stay close to home and stay close to you (because you too will be taking the day off as well). You will all feel better for it.

## WIDOWS WEAR STILETTOS "HEART MONITOR"
### "I'm Not Going Anywhere...I Promise!"

Three weeks after Mike's death, I underwent emergency abdominal surgery. This surgery was not life-threatening in any way; nevertheless, my daughter Kendall did not handle my going into the hospital at all well. She was in fact, in near hysterics, as she was quite convinced that Mommy was also going to die. I had an awful time convincing Kendall that Mommy was going to be just great and back home in six days with a sore belly and a craving for cheesecake.

Regardless of the age of your children, their foundation has been shaken to its very core. Daddy was the "rock", the "man of the house", the "protector"…and now he isn't here. The first and most "logical" fear that your children will express is that something will also happen to you. This fear is most likely to arise if you wrestle with any kind of illness or surgery soon after the death—or it may arise as soon as your children hear you sneeze!

Obviously, you cannot tell your children that "nothing is ever going to happen to you"—that's unrealistic and dishonest. However, I do believe in going with the odds that say in all likelihood, you are going to be around for a very long time and I feel these sentiments should be just fine to share with your children. However, this would not be the time for the "Everyone Has to Die Someday" speech. Don't guarantee your children that you are immortal; simply reassure them that you are here for them and you are here to stay.

More than anything else, your children are looking for that strong, reassuring foundation once again. Your children need to know that you can be counted on and that all of you are going to be just fine—even if you don't quite believe it today, you must instill that confidence in your children. Remember when we discussed the art of compartmentalizing? This will be one those times when your grief gets "put away" until a little later on.

## They CAN Handle the Truth!

As with any trauma, our initial instinct as parents is to shield our children from pain and trial. I have come to believe this to be a mistake. I'll also freely admit to having made this mistake in the past. An attempt to "shield" your children, distract them from what's going on, say that "everything is fine" when it is clearly not fine, will ultimately result in an elevated anxiety level. In other words, "What is Mom hiding from me?"

In helping your children through all of the transitions and with all of the questions that they are going to have after their father's death, the key words that you are going to want to remember are "age-appropriate". Do not offer more information than what is requested and keep the information limited to what children are able to comprehend. For example, a five-year-old may not necessarily need every single detail surrounding the death. Parents generally will imbue their spiritual beliefs here; for example, letting their children know that, "Daddy is in Heaven watching us now and even though we can't see him, he can see us and he loves us." When children ask if Daddy is coming back, you must answer honestly, but let them know that Daddy still loves them and always will.

Older children may express fears that concern not only you and your well-being, but matters such as the condition of the family finances and the future security of the family, now that Dad is no longer here. With older children, obviously there can be more honest and frank discussions. Again, they are looking for strength and reassurance and I'm all for giving it to them. Will you have to fake it at times? You'd better believe it. However, security and stability are our children's birthright and for that very reason, it becomes our responsibility to provide accordingly.

## Rally the "Troops"

One of the first things that you can do after your husband's passing to help reinforce your children's security is to inform everyone who impacts your children's lives on a regular basis as to what has occurred and that your children will need a lot of additional compassion and understanding. This includes, but is not limited to, your children's teachers; school psychologists or counselors; your family doctor or children's pediatrician; athletic coaches; religious instructors and/or leaders. The goal here is to create a visible and strong "network" of support for the children, so that whenever they feel overwhelmed or angry or just plain sad, children know that there are several directions in which they can turn.

Of utmost importance is continuing to stay in close contact with your child's teachers. Your child is going to need practical assistance with missed schoolwork (since the child will have taken time away from school during the period of mourning) as well as emotional support while he or she is at school and away from you.

## Don't Do This Alone, the Sequel (or, "Stop, Look and Listen")

Just as sorrow and depression can manifest in adults in the list of symptoms discussed in chapter 1 ("There's a Light at the End of the Tunnel"), so, too, may similar symptoms manifest with your child.

With a young child (age ten years and under), you will want to be on the lookout for any combination of the following:

Bedwetting

Nightmares/Night terrors

Overly aggressive behavior toward classmates, teammates, etc.

Tantrums

Withdrawal

Lack of appetite (absent physical illness)

Lack of interest in activities

Separation anxiety from mother and/or siblings

Disciplinary difficulties/"Acting out"

Your doctor or pediatrician will have many suggestions to help your child cope with his or her feelings of anger, sorrow and helplessness. Just as if the child had a throat infection or a broken leg, your child needs help—don't be afraid to get it! Jump on this *immediately*; don't wait for your child to "get over it" or hope that "it will go away with time." These are signs that your young child is in pain.

In pre-teen and adolescent children, watch for any of these symptoms:

Lack of appetite (again, absent physical illness)

Lack of interest in friends and activities

Withdrawal

Rebellion (disrespect for house rules, siblings, authority, etc.)

Physical violence/fighting

Destructive or reckless behavior (alcohol, drugs, smoking, driving carelessly, etc.)

Promiscuity/Irresponsible or indifferent attitude toward sex

Lawbreaking—ANY lawbreaking (there's no such thing as a "minor" law)

Truancy

Falling grades

Unreasonable separation anxiety from mother (yes, it *does* happen in older children!)

Withdrawal/Anti-social tendencies

Suicidal ideation (and there's no such thing as, "I wasn't really serious")

Should any of these behaviors become evident in your children, act immediately! Again, do not assume that "it's just a phase", "it's hormones", "she's just sad right now, she'll snap out of it" or "he's just being a boy". All these behaviors are desperate cries for help—don't ignore these cries! Immediately contact your family doctor or pediatrician, school psychologist or therapist—and enlist the expert's help! Let your children know that you are paying attention, you love them desperately, you take their pain seriously and you will do whatever it takes to lift them up and provide help through their suffering.

Some children may initially resist your seeking help for them, instead telling you that they are "handling it" or that "everything is fine". Seek help anyway—if you don't win the Most Popular Parent Award because you sought help on behalf of your children, who cares? It is far more important that your children know that you are paying attention, that you do care and that while it's okay to be angry, sad and depressed, not only are certain behaviors not going to bring Dad back or make things better, but also destructive behaviors of any kind are NOT going to be tolerated!

## CRY AND CARRY ON

I believe that one of the most difficult things on earth is to bear witness to our child's pain and heartache—especially when you feel helpless to do anything about it. This can be compounded by potential feelings of failure—that you've somehow failed as a parent, because your children are having a dreadful time and it's manifesting in disturbing fashions. All of this is multiplied tenfold because of the fact that you are still in mourning yourself.

Please know that you are not a failure. In addition to all of the other juggling acts that you are performing right now, you are also moving into another new role—that of the single parent. Please be patient with yourself. You have not failed your children. Let them know constantly that you are there for them and that you will help them in any and every way that you are capable—and then make sure that you do so!

### Nights are Forever...and Not in a Good Way

Just as you may find it difficult to sleep peacefully at night, so then may your children experience the same difficulty. That's when the "ghosties" come out, our household "code word" for when the mind—and imagination—go into overdrive. All of the anger, the fears and the emotions will inevitably choose nighttime to emerge.

Particularly with younger children, it is absolutely normal to experience a regression of sorts, in that they may express desires to sleep with their siblings or with you. You must obviously consider the ages and genders of your children in deciding whether or not this is appropriate to your household.

After her dad's death, Kendall expressed the need to sleep with me and

I indulged her, knowing that given time, she would willingly return to her own bed in her own room. Sure enough, as life slowly began to resume and a normal routine began to emerge in the house, Kendall went back to her own room of her own volition, feeling much more safe and secure.

If your children are younger, they may very well seek comfort in being permitted to sleep with siblings or with you (if practical) for a short time. However, if a substantial amount of time passes and a child does not seem inclined to resume sleeping in his own room and/or on his own, you will want to consult with his physician or pediatrician.

## It's a Mommy—It's a Daddy—It's SUPERPARENT!

I wish I had a dime for every time I heard the phrase, "Now I have to be a mother *and* a father. I don't know how to be both."

It's simple. You're not going to be "both". You are not "Daddy"—and you never will be. Simply stated, Mom is not Dad. Dad throws the football or baseball around or challenges us to a game of "hoops" and is typically the household "do-it-yourselfer" and the coach of the soccer team. Dad helps build snowmen, teaches you how to "partner dance" and has those big strong arms in which to wrap you up. Dad congratulates his sons on their gorgeous dates, while simultaneously swearing that his daughters won't date until they reach the age of thirty-five. So, while you will never be Dad, what you *can* do and what you can *strive* to be is the best mom of which you are capable of being.

Being a single parent (and a widowed parent at that) is definitely a role for which none of us signed on. It is both a constant challenge and (eventually) an incredible blessing. Your children will come to view you as heroic, for as they mature into this new future that you share, they will understand the role that you have been compelled to fill in their lives and love and appreciate you all the more for your efforts.

It isn't always easy though.

It can be quite difficult for the child who is functioning in a world where "everyone has a dad except me." Even children of divorced parents generally have a father somewhere and usually have a relationship of some sort with him.

I sought to reinforce Kendall with positive male role models in her life; not only male relatives but also most notably two "uncles" who are actually close family friends who love and care for her as if she were their own. I also made sure that she continued to counsel with our rabbi, who had counseled her for years through her dad's illness. To this day, these are the role models to whom she knows she can turn both in times of celebration and in times of trial. Seek out the same for your children. These models of support could be anyone from relatives to coaches—people whose judgment you trust implicitly and whom you know will care for and about your child as you do.

## CRY AND CARRY ON

There are inevitably going to be times when there truly is no substitute for Daddy…not even Mommy. One primary example would be the father-child activities that take place at school and with club or sports organizations.

Since Kendall was eleven years old at the time of her dad's death, she never had the opportunity to attend the annual "Father-Daughter" dance in high school. She was always a bit gloomy when the event was announced each year—especially because her daddy was the consummate dancer. She elected not to take a male relative, as for her, it would only have magnified her dad's absence. I then decided to make it a point to take her out each year on the evening of the dance. One year, we went to the beach for dinner; another year, we got all dressed up and went to a fine restaurant. Did it take the place of attending the dance with her daddy? Absolutely not. However, it did certainly buoy her spirits and subsequently became a Girls' Night tradition each year on the night that the dance took place.

### "I Know How You Feel" (Well, Not Really)

Four months after Mike died, I lost my father very suddenly to an aggressive form of cancer (it was admittedly a tough time). After our family gathered and arrangements were made, Kendall and I went out for a salad; one of our

Girl Traditions that is part of our "alone time". As we were eating and trying to absorb the enormity of death happening to us yet *again*, Kendall remarked, "Now you understand what I've been going through, because you've lost your daddy, too."

I thought for a moment about this sweet gesture of comfort from my daughter before I answered, "No Kendall, I really don't know what you're going through."

Remember in chapter 2 ("People Say the Dumbest Things") when someone may have told you that he or she understands how you feel? The fact is that unless the person is a young widow, he or she does *not* understand how you feel; rather, that person is recalling past grief in his or her life to try and relate to you. Keeping this in mind, I replied to Kendall, "It hurts very much to lose a parent (it did then and does to this day), but that's what happens when you are an adult. It's very sad, but parents eventually grow old and they pass away. My daddy was here when I was eleven years old and he was alive through my whole growing up. I didn't have to go through losing my daddy until now and I'm forty-one years old. I think that it must be much harder to lose a daddy when you're eleven years old. So I really don't know what you're going through."

After thinking about it for a moment, Kendall not only agreed, she also deeply appreciated the reply; the acknowledgment that as much pain as I was in, what she had to endure was in many ways so much more difficult.

As your children move through the loss of their father, you too must remember that unless you suffered the death of a parent at a young age, you do not know what they are going through any more than they can relate to what *you* are going through. Each has his or her own perspective on this situation, since all of the relationship dynamics are different. While it's fine to let your children know that you understand their loss, make sure that you *differentiate* their loss from your own and recognize that while you hurt, their loss too is of great magnitude.

Do not simply tell your children that you "know how they feel," because, in reality, you don't. You have lost a husband and although their father and your spouse are the same person, the loss *experience* and the loss *perspectives* are quite different. Instead, offer comfort and your ever-ready shoulder on which to cry or ear into which to talk. Please do not play "Who's Hurting The Most" with your children. It is to no advantage to try to "compete" as to who is in the most pain. There are no "winners". Both the wife and children are devastated; each in his or her own way. Don't make your children feel as though their pain is "less" or that your life is so much harder than their lives will be as a result of your loved one's death.

## Motherhood or "Smotherhood"?

We have already learned that in a period of intense grief, rather than act, we instead tend to react. You will quickly see that I was no different.

---

### WIDOWS WEAR STILETTOS LAUGH-O-METER

When Mike was initially diagnosed, we realized that his was a terminal illness and that whatever time we had left together, it was going to be quite limited. I then made the oh-so-brilliant decision that with the exception of work or taking our daughter Kendall to and from school, I was never again going to leave the house. Ever. I was instead going to sit on the couch, stare at Mike and wait for the inevitable.

One day, he finally had enough. In a manner that was uniquely Mike, he looked at me and said, "Quit staring at me like I'm about to explode. I'm not going to explode. You have got to get out of here, because you're driving me crazy."

You have my permission to laugh, because we certainly did.

---

After Mike's death, I reacted in the exact same manner as I had when Mike was diagnosed—except this time, with my daughter. I wanted to spend every waking hour with Kendall—and she wanted to spend the sleeping hours with me. This pretty much covered the twenty-four-hour span of the day. As much as she was reluctant to be away from me, I, too, hated the thought of being away from her, save the time that we had to be apart for work and school.

Without realizing it, we were slowly driving each other nuts.

As much as your children love you—and they do—they need time away from you as well. They need time with their friends, with their activities or to be alone in their rooms with their private pursuits; whether they are coloring books, playing video games, making telephone calls or listening to music that is, of course, too loud (as in, "turn that damn thing down" or "you call that music?").

As tempting as it is in this time of pain to smother our children with love, kindness, reinforcement, tenderness and all of the things that we know them to need, so, too, must we recognize that their normal lives must resume—and we must allow that resumption to occur! It is just as important to know when to "back away" as it is to be the reassuring presence that they need as well.

Just as your children need time away from you—guess what? You need time away from them too! If they are not old enough to stay by themselves, hire a babysitter or contact a relative to hang out with them for a few hours. Then grab a friend or two and go to lunch, dinner, cocktails or shopping—any activity that does not require you to be taking care of someone. Give yourself permission to take off the Mommy/Daddy hat for just a little while. In chapter 3 ("Thinking 'Inside the Box'"), we studied the art of compartmentalizing—and here is where you get to practice that newly-learned art. Jump into the "girlfriend" compartment and go!

You and your children will go through many changes as all of you progress on your journey of healing and recovery. Be open to one another; be kind and understanding to each other—even youngsters will grasp this concept. As time passes, be assured that you will see new parent-child relationships evolve; ones that are stronger and more tightly-knit than you could have ever imagined. I wish so much love and happiness to you and your "babies"(and they *are* your babies, regardless of their ages!)—and I promise that you will be rewarded abundantly with both.

### WIDOWS WEAR STILETTOS "HEART MONITOR"

As you did in chapter 1 ("There's a Light at the End of the Tunnel"), return to the list of feelings earlier in this chapter. Understanding that your children may have experienced all of these feelings at some point, select the **five** feelings or behaviors that you feel are affecting your children the most or that you believe they are dealing with on a daily or regular basis:

_____

_____

_____

_____

Are there "trigger mechanisms" for these feelings or behaviors that you are able to identify? If so, list them here:

_____

_____

_____

_____

**(For children ages eight years and above)** Cover your previous answers. Have your children review the list in this chapter and write down the top five feelings that they feel are affecting their daily lives or with which they believe they are dealing with on a daily or regular basis:

_____

_____

_____

_____

Compare your answers. Have your children written down feelings of which you were unaware? Did you write down behaviors that they didn't realize they were exhibiting? Next, write down any differences—and then use these lists to invite dialogue between you and your children as to how the death of their father is affecting them:

_____

_____

_____

_____

---

## FROM THE STILETTO FILE

If your children are too young to take part in these exercises, you can still invite important dialogue by making sure that you are creating an environment where they feel free to talk about Daddy. Pay close attention to the list of feelings/behaviors that can affect younger children and if you are unable to resolve or relieve these symptoms on your own, enlist the help of your pediatrician immediately.

---

Go back and review the section on "Rally the Troops" in this chapter. Who will you enlist as positive male role models for your child(ren)? Remember, this is in no way meant as a "Daddy Replacement", because there will be no such thing. However, the presence of positive male influences in your children's lives will serve to reinforce them on their healing journeys:

_____

_____

_____

_____

Decide on and plan a family event or outing with you and all of your children together. This can be your upcoming family vacation or something as simple as a picnic, trip to the beach or an amusement park; and yes, make older children a part of this as well. The objective is to give **all** of you something positive to look forward to and take part in together as a family. Everyone (regardless of age!) gets to make one suggestion for an activity and the entire family can choose from the list:

_____

_____

_____

_____

As you will learn in the next chapter, there will be moments of pain and challenges as you all continue to move forward on your healing journeys. However, as we've also gone over earlier in this chapter, open dialogue, continued communication and sensitivity to your children and their needs to grieve will not only bring all of you together as a unit, but will also strengthen all of you on the "challenging" days.

### Chapter 9

# THE "FIRSTS"—PART I
## (On the Calendar)

At the risk of sounding trite, the "firsts" are the worst. What are the "firsts"? These are the occasions, large and small, that must be faced for the first time without your husband. These include, but are certainly not limited to, the first of *any* of the major holidays (secular and religious); the first Mother's and Father's Days; the first wedding anniversary and the first birthdays (yours, his *and* your children's).

Through my own healing process, I have discovered that there are actually two separate and distinct kinds of "firsts". There are the "firsts" that show up on the calendar, in the malls and in the greeting card stores— the major holidays that completely surround you everywhere. There are then the "firsts" that are not "holidays" so much as they are significant first-time events after the death.

One of the first things that will cross your mind after your husband's death, if it hasn't already, is, "How am I going to survive the 'firsts', any of them?"

The answer is, you do.

Though the pain of loss and the glaring absence of your spouse will certainly be with you, there are ways to make these "firsts" not just bearable, but that can actually help you develop new traditions of remembrance. Since we have no control over the calendar and because Christmas and Hanukkah decorations appear in the stores shortly after the Fourth of July, we begin with the "firsts" on the calendar.

## The "Big Ones"

When it comes to Christmas, Hanukkah, Easter and other holidays that directly involve children or presents and general merriment, you will instinctively put your own feelings aside in the interest of the children's celebration. Depending on when the death occurred, the holiday may be somewhat subdued, but it should not be ignored entirely.

---

### FROM THE STILETTO FILE

Mike died six days before Christmas and squarely in the middle of Hanukkah. Honestly, I didn't know what was appropriate under the circumstances, so I consulted with our rabbi. He suggested that we light the Hanukkah candles and recite prayers, but that we shouldn't attend the annual Hanukkah party at synagogue, play dreidl (a game traditionally played at Hanukkah) or engage in other festivities at home. During the holiday, we took quiet walks around the neighborhood looking at all of the Christmas lights and decorations of the season, but did not attend any holiday parties of any kind. At the invitation of the general manager at our very favorite fine dining restaurant, we enjoyed a quiet and wonderful dinner on New Year's Eve. She saw to it that we dined very early in the evening and were able to leave well before any of the dancing and partying began.

We found these activities were perfect for us in the early grieving period; the holidays were observed, but the *gaiety* of the season was curtailed.

---

There are several other good reasons for continuing forward with holiday observances and the most important would be to demonstrate to your children that life will continue. Younger children in particular will need to know that just because Daddy isn't in the living room doesn't mean that Santa Claus or Easter Bunny has forgotten them, or that Hanukkah or Kwanzaa shouldn't be commemorated. I feel this is good advice on how to handle birthdays and other holidays, which should be celebrated appropriately, according to the age of the celebrant and the proximity to the death of your husband.

---

## FROM THE STILETTO FILE

On my first birthday after Mike's death, which was three months after his passing, I elected to have a quiet dinner at a lovely French restaurant with my mother and Kendall. However, on Kendall's first birthday after Mike's death (six months after Mike's passing), we had a combination sixth grade graduation/twelfth birthday slumber party. Filled with wonderfully giggly pre-adolescent girls, extremely loud pop music and requisite junk food, our house was a noisy, riotous good time; particularly because Kendall had been unable to have any sleepovers or childhood parties throughout Mike's illness.

Celebrating Kendall's birthday in this manner was wonderfully fitting—for her. Celebrating my birthday quietly, however, was necessary for me.

---

The first Father's Day after your husband's passing will likely be very difficult for your children as well as for you. This would be a good time to encourage them to offer their fondest or funniest "Daddy Memories" on that holiday and believe me, this activity works regardless of age. If you traditionally went out to brunch or dinner on Father's Day (as we did), by all means go; go out to Dad's favorite restaurant and order his favorite drink or favorite appetizer to share. Did you stay at home and barbeque instead? Do it! Play charades or Pictionary? That's better still, you can get really silly! It can be a poignant day of fond memories, rather than a day filled with sadness and emptiness.

## CRY AND CARRY ON

There is no denying that the first wedding anniversary after the loss of your husband is difficult to handle. This occasion is one of the most painful reminders of your status as a new widow; yet you are entitled to commemorate the occasion, should you chose to do so.

I chose to look at our wedding pictures (rather than the video), open a bottle of champagne and toast our marriage that lasted forever. Granted, "forever" wasn't very long for us, but we were, in fact, married "till death do us part" and how many couples can say that nowadays? Was it difficult to commemorate under the circumstances? You'd better believe it. Worth remembering? Indeed.

There will be other difficult "firsts" during that initial year of widowhood—holidays that were especially meaningful to you, special family commemorations, anniversaries or events. My daughter and I chose to remember each and every holiday, birthday and anniversary with some kind of celebration or observance. Yes, of course there will be tears, but eventually, the tears will be through the smiles of warm memories.

As tough as these "firsts" might be, you can also believe me when I say that after the year of the "firsts", each subsequent year that passes becomes easier to bear. In the following years, holidays and special occasions will once again be something to look forward to with anticipation, rather than dread. For example, on what would have been our tenth wedding anniversary, I returned to the place where Mike and I were married—a beautiful spot overlooking a lake—and had a picnic all by myself. I remembered with a smile (as well as a few tears) the joy of our wedding day, the fabulous reception that ensued and how we were surrounded by so much love that day.

## Once in a Lifetime

Events such as weddings, graduations and other lifetime milestones definitely will illuminate the absence of your spouse. Here is where you can be inventive, involve your children and create special ways to make your late husband's memory a part of the festivities.

When Kendall became Bat Mitzvah, her daddy had been gone for about a year and a half. This was a particularly poignant time as after his initial diagnosis, one of the very first things that Mike had expressed was his fervent desire to live to see Kendall's special day arrive. I knew that Kendall was feeling her daddy's loss acutely during what was supposed to be one of the most joyous milestones in her life. It was up to us to make Mike as much a part of the day as possible—we simply could not allow it to be a day riddled with sadness.

Of course, Mike was remembered during the actual Bat Mitzvah ceremony—both by the rabbi and in Kendall's speech to the congregation. For the reception that evening, we had created a "Daddy Table", which featured a collage of some of Kendall's favorite pictures of her and her daddy together, along with two blue and white candles, his mounted unit cowboy hat and police badge, a small bottle of Jack Daniels (Mike's favorite tipple) and a glass turned upside down (a tradition among police officers in acknowledging those who are absent). This was accompanied by a framed letter authored by Kendall, dedicating her special day to Daddy. Mike was remembered once again during the traditional candle lighting ceremony, while the song "Atomic Dog" by the great George Clinton played in the background—a funny, lovely and obvious nod to Mike's career as a K-9 police officer and cowboy.

These were all fitting and uplifting tributes to Mike's memory and while everyone in attendance shed more than a few tears, at the same time, we were truly able to celebrate the day in the manner that Kendall deserved—and in the way that Mike himself most certainly would have demanded!

Even though nothing can or ever will replace the absence of your husband and your children's father during times of great celebration, there are so many ways to honor and celebrate his memory. Use your imagination…create a "Daddy Table" at a wedding reception or graduation party; play a favorite song; include a picture collage; serve a favorite dish. It will bring smiles to faces and make the absence a little easier to bear.

## JUST FOR YOU

### Party On?

Do not force your children to attend parties if they are not yet in the party spirit. Under this particular set of circumstances, please do not decide what you believe to be "best" for them. Would you want someone forcing you to go out and "have a good time" when your heart is too heavy to do so? Probably not and the same goes for your children.

On the other hand, if your children are "right and ready" for socializing soon after the death, don't be shocked or judgmental. Some deal with grief more productively when they are around others in a positive situation. Above all, remember that your children are not merely an extension of you. They have feelings and coping mechanisms of their own and those feelings must be respected.

When it comes to the major holidays, such as Thanksgiving, Christmas, New Year's Eve and Easter, regardless of when the death occurred, those closest to you will want to include you in parties and gatherings and may even try to talk you into celebrating—but you may just not be "there" yet. Even though holidays and special occasions will have a more subdued feeling about them at first, with the passing of time comes the return of rejoicing.

Most importantly, tune into you and your children. Don't feel like any of you have to "celebrate" or be "on" if you don't feel like it, especially if the proximity of the occasion is very close to when the death occurred. Give yourself permission to say "no" to attending parties, gatherings or situations where you would be uncomfortable—it's absolutely all right to do so.

## WIDOWS WEAR STILETTOS "HEART MONITOR"

Let's look at your calendar.

• What holiday(s) and/or occasions (such as birthdays or an anniversary) are coming up with which you feel that you (and/or your children) may have a difficult time observing?

_____

_____

_____

_____

_____

• Go back to your list and put a star by the one holiday or occasion that you feel will be the most difficult for you (and/or your children) to endure.

• Enlisting the suggestions and ideas of your children (if they are old enough to talk, they are old enough to have suggestions and ideas!), list different and positive ways that your husband's memory can be made a part of the holiday or occasion. Get creative and have a little bit of fun here—remember, it's okay to make this fun. Examples might include hanging his favorite ornaments on your Christmas tree or the creation of a small "Daddy" tree that includes ornaments and photographs displayed on it; a special menorah that your children can light "for Daddy"; the inclusion of his favorite holiday dishes at the meal, as the next "Stiletto File" illustration demonstrates.

_____

_____

_____

_____

_____

_____

_____

_____

## FROM THE STILETTO FILE

Everyone is familiar with the green bean casserole with the crunchy fried onion topping that has about eighty jillion calories, no real redeeming nutritional value and is sinfully, delightfully DELICIOUS. In our home, Mike made this dish for virtually every single major holiday. Now, regardless of whatever else is served at our holiday feasts, Mike's green bean casserole (prepared either by myself or by Kendall) is on the table as well. Believe it or not, you will be pleasantly surprised at how much comfort something as simple as featuring a favorite dish or dessert at the holiday meal will bring to you.

• Do you have special "once-in-a-lifetime" celebrations (such as a wedding, Bar/Bat Mitzvah, confirmation or graduation ceremony) coming up, of which your husband would have been an integral part? List those occasions here:

_____

_____

_____

_____

• List some of the ways that the memory of your husband can be honored in a meaningful and uplifting way. Examples might include a "Daddy Table", which you read about earlier in the chapter, inclusion of a favorite food, drink or music during the celebration or a photo or video montage set to music and prominently displayed.

_____

_____

_____

_____

Getting through the "firsts" on the calendar is difficult, without question. However, as you can also see by reading over your lists of celebration plans and ideas, they don't have to be unbearably painful. They can also be times for smiles and laughter (even through tears) while surrounding yourself with warm memories of wonderful times past.

With all of the "firsts" that you have encountered in this chapter and that you will continue to encounter in your new life, did you also know that there are even more "firsts" that you are going to face—"firsts" that may have never even occurred to you! Whether you are blissfully unaware or otherwise, like it or not, those "firsts" will be coming at you, my friend.

Now, let's help you get ready for....

### Chapter 10

# THE "FIRSTS"—PART II
**(Definitely Not on the Calendar!)**

Holidays or events which occur in the early weeks and months after your husband's death are definitely normal and reasonable concerns. However, sooner or later, whatever your personal timeline, the reality exists that as a young widow, you are going to meet someone whom you find attractive. What's more, that person may very well find you attractive too! This is going to lead you into a whole new area of "firsts" and a whole plethora of brand new feelings with which to deal. We're now going to examine these "firsts", beginning with your re-entry into the World of Women and Men.

## WIDOWS WEAR STILETTOS LAUGH-O-METER

Several months after Mike's death, I was in sudden need of medical attention. Between the fact that I was a brand new widow and that I needed to see a physician, I was hardly concerned with my appearance at that point in time. I dressed in a manner that could only be described as haphazard at best, my hair carelessly was stuck into a ponytail, my face was devoid of any makeup and I was wearing an old oversized sweater and sweat pants. Visually speaking, I was hardly the Diva Goddess that I like to imagine myself (or at least strive to be), but remember, I was not feeling very well either.

I was waiting patiently in the examining room when in walked the doctor by whom I had never before been treated. He was, without a doubt, one of the most breathtakingly gorgeous men I had seen in a very long time. Worse yet, he was funny, charming and intelligent. There I was expecting some old, bald guy and in walks someone right out of GQ.

Wonderful. Don't tell me that God doesn't have a sense of humor.

For the first time in a very long time, I was acutely aware of my appearance (or lack thereof). I didn't want him to look directly at me, out of fear of doing further damage to my pride or to his retinas. I was so disconcerted by these sudden feelings of—dare I say it—ATTRACTION. I literally didn't know what to do or say. I felt guilty and ashamed, as though I were cheating on Mike, my daughter, my family, my friends, my work colleagues, my country, you name it.

After I left the doctor's office—and by "left", I mean *bolted*, head-down, with my hand over my eyes—I immediately called my rabbi (from the parking lot, no less) and demanded to know what was wrong with me. My husband was dead for mere *months* and here I am finding men attractive? I was worried about what I looked like? What in *hell* was the matter with me???

Imagine my total shock when I was told that absolutely *nothing* was wrong with me.

Later, this actual *rational* person explained to me with a solid sense of objectivity that, in reality and due to the nature of my husband's illness, I had "lost" my husband long before he died. So while I had been a widow for a very short time chronologically, in a greater sense, I had been without my husband, as I knew him in that role, for a good deal longer. He went on to say that my feeling attracted to another man and being worried about my appearance was actually a *good* thing, rather than something about which to feel guilty!

Lesson learned: An expert opinion can be helpful!

## I'm Widowed, Not Contagious (or He's Gone, I'm Not!)

One of the things that Mike worried about the most was my desire to "go find love again" (his words) after he was gone. He told me over and over that I was "too young and too beautiful" (again, his words) to "jump into the grave" with him and that once he was no longer with us, I immediately needed to go out into the world in the determined pursuit of new love. His concern was so great that unbeknownst to me, he actually discussed this subject at great length with my mother.

I asked him if I could take some time off first. We both laughed.

Long before I was ever widowed, I had been divorced (my marriage to Mike was my second). Sadly, this is not an uncommon occurrence in our society today, so in the past, when I told people that I had been divorced, it was never a huge deal. Many years later, when I became widowed, I naively thought that telling people that I was a widow would show strength of character and integrity, that I was someone who had been deeply in love and committed to another and that we remained loving and loyal to one another "till death did we part". I thought I was a walking résumé for anyone who was looking for a partner who could be counted on in the rough times, who didn't cut and run when the going got tough and who was a woman of her word—that even though "forever" hadn't been very long for us, I had been, in fact, married "forever". Plus, in my mind, it beat the hell out of being a "bitter divorcee".

I could not have been more wrong.

## WIDOWS WEAR STILETTOS LAUGH-O-METER

After my husband's death, my first foray back into the "world of the social" was five months later at a synagogue function. While I was enjoying being back out and among friends, I met a man who appeared to be attracted to me—that is, until he inquired as to my marital status. When I told him that I was widowed, he PHYSICALLY took two steps BACKWARD. He literally backed away from me!

The first words that came into my mind (and out of my mouth before I could stop myself) were, "Really, it's not contagious."

Didn't see him the rest of the evening…and that was fine with me.

As time passed upon meeting other men, I occasionally received very similar reactions when mentioning the fact that I was a widow. For the longest time, I couldn't figure out why being a widow drew such a negative reaction. In my mind (and according to my birth certificate and on good days, the mirror in my bathroom), I still was young, energetic, fun-loving, social, enthusiastic…all of the attributes that I thought men would find somewhat desirable.

Puzzled, I finally asked a dear and trusted male friend of mine, what is up with this nonsense? I clean up pretty well (and have the clothes bills to prove it), I'm reasonably intelligent, I'm well-educated and I don't have a social disease (big plus there). Am I wearing Man Repellant No. 5? Am I a toad, complete with warts? I thought that as opposed to being "divorced and bitter", being widowed would demonstrate all of the aforementioned simply wonderful things about wonderful me and who wouldn't want to date wonderful me?

Why, then, are people backing away from me?

I could tell that my friend was struggling to choose his words carefully. He finally replied, "Well…there's a lot of baggage there."

(In my head echoed the words, "Um…excuse me, my late husband is not a suitcase.")

Then it dawned on me…and the clouds parted and I heard angels singing; kind of like what you hear in your head when you find the perfect pair of four-inch black strappy sandals that don't hurt your feet. Everyone is either intimidated by or is afraid of competing with:

## THE GHOST OF HUSBAND PAST

No, I haven't gone all otherworldly and we will discuss the concept of "baggage" further in chapter 12, entitled, "Now You'll Have Closure (And Other Myths Laid to Rest)". Be aware however, that there is a "ghost" that sits at our dining room table, at your dining room table and the dining room table of every other widow in the world.

It's the Ghost of Husband Past.

Unlike divorce, where chances are excellent that you would rather just forget ever having been married to your "ex", the Ghost of Husband Past apparently *never* did anything wrong! His passing has elevated him to something akin to sainthood. He *never* left the toilet seat up, he *never* left the gas tank on empty for you to fill, he *always* called when he was going to be late, he *never* left his dirty underwear on the bathroom floor or hogged the remote control or needed the bedroom window wide open at night in January.

Yeah, right. Back to reality now…

Somehow, the "mystique" that surrounds death leads absolutely everyone to believe that the Ghost of Husband Past was perfect in every way and anyone that comes along after the Ghost of Husband Past will never measure up or so some men believe.

And that's not all. Some men also believe that you either are or should be wearing a permanent black veil and that you will never want to be with or talk about any other man ever in your entire life. Even if you did, no other man could possibly ever measure up—emotionally, spiritually, romantically or intimately—to the Ghost of Husband Past. Your life is now about building shrines, waxing nostalgic and somehow or another, your life ended with his, it's just that *you're still here.*

Please don't worry. I promise you that there really *are* men out there who will not view you or your widowed marital status as a duffel bag.

These same men will not think that they will catch a severe case of Death as a result of being in your space for an extended period of time. There is, however, the invisible "standard" by which a new man in your life may feel that he will be measured and it's going to be up to you to dispel that notion and do it quickly.

For example, remember those wedding rings that you were wondering about moving to your right hand or removing altogether? If you're still wearing your rings on your left hand, whether you realize it or not, that's one of the "yardsticks" being waved in a man's face, the constant reminder of the "perfect" Ghost of Husband Past and this is something that you will want to take into consideration as you venture forth back into the World of Women and Men.

---

### CAROLE'S "COMEBACK" CORNER

When I meet someone new and the person inquires about my marital status, I reply that I'm widowed. He will immediately respond that he's sorry, to which I say, "Thank you, I appreciate that." If he asks me with what illness Mike was afflicted, I will tell him. That's it. I answer what is asked and that's all. Only if there are subsequent conversations or dates or if a friendship or relationship of any kind ensues, will I elaborate further. That is, of course, when my new friend's confidence and comfort levels are firmly established. In other words, you must let him know that your husband is gone and while that is a tragedy and you will always miss him and have love in your heart for him, you are still here, moving forward with your life and you're happy to be doing so—maybe even with someone like him!

The whole process of re-entering the dating world as a widow is rather like "testing" a bruise to see if it still hurts. Have you ever had a really nasty, awful-looking bruise? What's the first thing that you do? You push on it—constantly. Even if you know it's going to hurt, you push on it to see if it still hurts and if so, how much!

Sometimes it looks like the bruise is all cleared up; yet when you push on the spot, it still smarts a bit. By the same token, there is an enormous bruise of sorts on your heart right now, as you have sustained one of the worst kinds of injuries imaginable. As with a bruise on your body, from time to time, push on that spot in your heart to see if it still hurts. If it's still painful…*quit pushing*! It means that it's not time for you to be dating yet! Believe me, just as with a bruise, eventually that sore and tender spot in your heart does heal—and so will you!

Let's go back to Dr. Gorgeous for a moment and my absolute horror at discovering that I was attracted to this man as well as the simple fact that, apparently, I was open to being attracted to any man period. Clearly, my heart and my spirit were open to new possibilities (even if that fact had not yet reached my brain!) and, to which my counselor and rabbi had awakened me, those new possibilities were actually reasons to celebrate. I had unknowingly (and surprisingly) taken a necessary first step into my new life.

## The First Date

You've met someone and for the first time since your husband's death, you are going to venture out, full of hope and expectation on a DATE! First of all, congratulations. This is an enormous step on your healing journey as a widow and a courageous step at that.

Suddenly, there you are, standing in front of your closet full of clothes and finding absolutely nothing to wear. You recite the well-known and ever-popular "Hair Prayer"…you know the one:

---

## CAROLE'S HAIR PRAYER

Dear Lord
If You make my hair turn out perfectly tonight,
I will never ever ask you for another thing as long as I live
Or at least until the next time that
I have to look totally deliciously fabulous.
Amen.

---

Naturally, no matter how great your hair turns out, it won't be right. Your hands are clammy and never mind butterflies—your stomach has bats in it. It's 10:00 in the morning and you find yourself wondering if you can lose ten pounds by 6:00 p.m. tonight.

Yup, it's a first date all right.

Later, there you are at a restaurant or coffeehouse, doing the "First Date Dance" that we've all done. You know: being cute and charming, sitting up straight, watching what you say, taking care to avoid food pitfalls like ordering spaghetti when wearing white, ordering nothing involving the words "spinach" or "garlic" (spinach winds up in teeth; garlic winds up on breath!) and never ordering spareribs (no good can come of that!). You catch yourself thinking, *The hell with this, I'd rather be on a date with Ben & Jerry (the ice cream, not the guys). After all, you aren't "supposed" to have to be doing this at your age; you're "supposed" to be married, right?*

...and you wonder if it's all worth it.

Let's get one thing straight right off. A first date with a new person under normal circumstances is nerve-wracking. The first date after the death of your husband is weird. Period. Chances are excellent that you haven't had to do the First Date Dance in a long time; that the last time you were out with a man, you ate off his plate and your conversation likely consisted of what was going on at the office or who was taking the dog to the veterinarian or that the carpets needed cleaning or the oil in the car needed changing—because it was your husband. This is now an entirely different situation and while not you're not "new" to dating as you were when you were a teenager, this is admittedly a new dating dynamic for you.

Possibly the most challenging part of the first date is to make the conversation about topics other than your status as a widow. Your date will naturally inquire about your husband's death and the surrounding circumstances, because as we know, young widows are a curiosity. I talk about my late husband with affection and a smile, but I did not choose that time to talk about how great he was or how amazing life was with him or how awful his illness was or how much I miss him.

Your date should not have to compete with the Ghost of Husband Past. Further, and as much as you may be tempted, you cannot bring the Ghost of Husband Past on dates with you: it's highly unfair to the man who found you intriguing and fabulous enough to ask you out (and is likely picking up the tab).

The best advice here is to RELAX and enjoy yourself! You are entitled. You have earned it. Let this person, who has had the great good sense and taste to ask you out, pamper and spoil you a little bit. It is through the dating process that you are also going to discover a side of you that is brand new—and even a little bit exciting!

## WIDOWS WEAR STILETTOS LAUGH-O-METER
### Liars and Tightwads and Boors—OH MY!

While it is not my wish to scare you, after a considerable amount of dating in the years since my husband's death, I can affirm and attest that jerks, idiots and emotionally stunted nitwits are still alive and well and thriving among us in the twenty-first century. Allow me then to introduce you to:

- **"Lied About My Age By Fifteen Years" Guy.**

(This is not an "age" issue: it's a lying issue. While we're at it, let's also include lying about marital status, appearance and gainful employment (or lack thereof). The obvious question here is—what else is he lying about? This is simple mathematics, guys: Lying About Anything = Game OVER.)

- **"I'm Almost Fifty Years Old And I Haven't Gotten Over My High School Sweetheart Who Dumped Me Decades Ago and Screwed Me Up For Life" Guy.**

(Try to keep a straight face while listening to that twaddle. It's not easy.)

- **"Name-Dropper" Guy (as in, "I Know Thus-and-Such Celebrity And I Can't Reveal Any Names So Don't Ask Me; I Belong To Thus-and-Such Exclusive Club; I Drive 'X-Brand' Car").**

(The assumption here is that I am either impressed or that I care.)

- **"I Have No Interest In What You're Saying Because I'd Rather Hear Myself Talk" Guy.**

(Did you ever get the feeling that if you suddenly jumped up, lit yourself on fire and started dancing naked with birch twigs, a guy like this wouldn't stop talking long enough to render a comment—or even take notice?)

- **"Proposes On The First Date" Guy.**

(Yes, the first date. Seriously. I swear I heard the song "Desperado" playing in my head.)

- **"Give Her the Bill, She Makes More Than I Do" Guy.**

(These words were spoken by the same guy who thought it was fine to take a flask into a restaurant and "mix his own" in order to protest the high cost of drinks. I'm all for social activism, but come on...)

And, of course, we simply *cannot* leave out the ever-popular:

- **"Swears That You're THE Perfect Woman And THE Greatest Thing That's Ever Happened To Him; Then Completely Vanishes Into Thin Air Overnight, Giving You Absolutely No Reason For Disappearing" Guy.**

(As have most women, I too have met a couple of these "gems". Take heart and trust me—**it isn't you**. And just for the record, not only do **they** know who they are, they also know that **WE** know who they are!)

I know—you're right now wondering if every single one of the guys on the Laugh-O-Meter has really happened to me. The answer is absolutely yes and I'll bet that at some point in your life, prior to or since marriage, at least one or two of them have happened to you, too. We all know that the guys whom I've just described have always and forever existed—this isn't exactly front-page news! If it was maddening dealing with guys like this before you met your husband, who would never do such things or behave in such a manner (!), it's even more frustrating now—remember, the Ghost of Husband Past was perfect!

Kidding aside and more importantly, though there are definitely guys whom you'll need and want to avoid out there, it's so worth every single "bad" date when you meet a new friend who might wind up being even more than a friend! Even with all of the not-so-fabulous dates that I have endured, I hasten to add that I have also met some absolutely wonderful men along the way: first-class, kind and decent men who have become trusted, dear and good friends and are an important part of my life.

Many women ask me if dating is "difficult", meaning since my husband's death. It can be sometimes, but not because of the fact that I'm a widow. Think back…wasn't dating difficult when you first began dating, however many years ago that may have been? The "hard part" hasn't changed much, but your perspective certainly will have changed. There truly is no substitute for experience!

## CRY AND CARRY ON

After the first date, or perhaps even the first few dates, you may feel overwhelmingly guilty; almost as though you're "cheating" on your late husband. We call this the "cheating twinges" and as demonstrated by my reaction upon meeting Dr. Gorgeous, none of us is immune to those "twinges". However, you must also remember that your husband is no longer alive and you are entitled to move forward into a new life—a life that includes companionship.

You may also feel downright angry with your late husband, because if he were still here, you wouldn't be in this position to begin with—more than likely, this is going to happen after a truly lousy date. That's perfectly normal too; if I've experienced a bad date (and given the aforementioned list of "winners", I obviously have!), I will come home and "talk it down" with Mike, whom I'm certain is somewhere watching closely and laughing—especially after the one completely wretched date where I actually bailed mid-drink, went out and bought brand new furniture for my living room.

Very expensive drink, that one!

### The First Meeting—of the Children

Inevitably, the question of introducing the children to dates comes up. Remember bringing dates home to meet your parents? It is about a hundred times more difficult to bring dates home to your children—talk about going before a jury!

Though there are those who may disagree, it is my strongest feeling that regardless of the ages of your children, you should *not* introduce them to every single man with whom you spend time. I feel that it is only when you have decided that you will be involved exclusively with one man that he should be introduced into the family dynamic, whether it's going on a family outing, attending a family event or even something as simple as picking you up at your home.

There is absolutely nothing wrong with dating more than one man at a time until or unless you choose to date one man exclusively. However, it will create confusion and a sense of uncertainty with your children if in their eyes, the front door becomes a "revolving door"—they won't know where or with whom to trust their emotions. Remember, they have lost Daddy and whether they voice it or not, they may view anyone to whom they are introduced as a potential "new Daddy".

## JUST FOR YOU

Another consideration is that, again, regardless of the ages of your children, be they toddlers or "all grown up", no matter how little or how much time has passed since their dad's death, they are going to have a challenging time assimilating the thought of you with another man; let alone actually seeing you laughing with, enjoying time with and being affectionate with another man. Tread carefully and sensitively here; this is not the time to "spring" surprises (i.e., bringing the man you're seeing home unannounced, before your children have had adequate time or notice to prepare emotionally). Before introducing a man to your children, sit down with them over a meal, turn off the television, put all telephones on "ignore" and discuss taking this step in your life with them.

When I began to date again, I made it very clear to Kendall that no matter with whom I chose to spend time or even possibly fall in love, no one ever could or would replace her daddy in my heart. We discussed that dating and/or falling in love with another man bore no reflection on my love for her dad, that it was time for me to continue forward with my life and that companionship is a normal and natural part of that continuity.

When the time was appropriate to introduce Kendall to my "First Love" (my first serious involvement subsequent to Mike's death), she understood all of this and she was prepared to meet and welcome the new man in my life with an open mind and a smile.

No matter how tempting, no matter how nice the person, even if he asks to meet the children, I recommend that until or unless you and he have established that yours will be an exclusive relationship, you should wait before you introduce your children into the situation.

## THE DATING GAME

So, how do you feel about re-entering the World of Women and Men? You may feel ready to get back into *The Dating Game*—or perhaps you want to with all of your heart, but you feel like something (the Ghost of Husband Past or Everyone Else or even your own mind) might be holding you back. Let's find out by checking in with your head and your heart. Keep in mind that there are no "right or wrong" answers here—we're just getting a "feel" for where you are in your recovery process and if you feel ready to take this next step—be honest with yourself!

Let's play the *Widows Wear Stilettos'* version of *The Dating Game*. Circle the answer that best applies to how you're feeling right now:

**1. It has been _____ since my husband died.**
    a. At least one year
    b. Six months to one year
    c. Less than six months

**2. At this point, the thought of dating makes me feel:**

a. Excited—I realize that while I will always have love in my heart for my husband, I'm ready to move forward and proud of myself for taking the next step.

b. A little bit nervous but if I take it slowly, I'm sure I'll be OK.

c. So incredibly sad and/or guilty that I cannot even think about it yet.

**3. When I think of myself in terms of possibly being affectionate with another man in public (flirting, holding hands, kissing, etc.), I feel:**

a. Ready—physical affection is perfectly acceptable.

b. That it's going to be kind of weird, but I would try to relax and "go with it" if that's where things seem to be headed.

c. Like Hank Williams' "Your Cheatin' Heart" ought to be playing in the background.

**4. As to my progress on my healing journey, I feel like:**

a. I'm either where I thought I would be or even further along than I thought I would be. I have my moments of course, but I know that's an absolutely normal part of the process.

b. I'm doing all right, but I still have quite a number of "bad days".

c. I can't even bring myself to go through his things…I'm just not there yet.

**5. Were I to tell my children (in a manner that is age-appropriate) that I was contemplating dating again, I would most likely be greeted with:**

a. Wholehearted support; perhaps even enthusiasm.

b. Some support, albeit tentative; they still struggle with their father's death on a regular basis, but want my happiness, too.

c. Tears, tantrums and/or a packed suitcase (either mine or theirs).

Now let's have a look at your answers, what they mean and after taking this quiz, how you should be approaching *The Dating Game*.

**If your answers are:**

**MOSTLY As:** You have reached a place of peace and contentment on your healing journey; a place where you are able to introduce dating into your lifestyle without feeling guilty or overwhelmingly sad. You recognize that like everything else on your journey, this too is an adjustment, but one for which you feel ready—and perhaps a little bit eager too. You have accepted that you will always love your husband, but that love is now in the proper perspective and you feel ready for new possibilities.

**MOSTLY Bs:** Even though you may feel that you're ready to begin dating and/or that you want to begin dating again, you may be in a place of transition right now—either with your own feelings, the feelings of your children or a combination of the two. Perhaps not quite enough time has passed or maybe you feel as though you are being "pushed along" on your healing journey by outside influences or opinions (you know…Everyone Else, who says that you should be "over it" and dating already!).

Consider also that it sometimes takes getting "out there" to discover whether or not the time is right for you to begin dating again. You need to closely examine your feelings and apart from any outside opinions or influences, ask yourself if you are truly ready for this step in your life. If not, that's absolutely fine—you owe no one any explanation or justification as to your feelings.

**MOSTLY Cs:** You have not **yet** (hold onto that word please!) reached that point in your healing where you really want to be dating—and that's okay. Back up and take some time off—and time out—for you! Once again, and as I've said several times, when the time is right, you will know.

If the prospect of dating is too difficult to you or you are not yet able to put your life with your husband in its proper perspective (which is not necessarily on a first date); if you spend entire conversations talking only of your late husband, the life you had together and the life you didn't get to have together; more importantly, if you speak of him more often with tears than with smiles, now is not the time for you to begin dating. Take out your calendar and commit to revisiting this quiz in six months to see if and how your feelings have changed.

## JUST FOR YOU

After playing *The Dating Game,* if you scored mostly "C" answers and, understanding that everyone has different healing timelines, we also want to make sure that you don't choose to stay in mourning for the rest of your life—that's not why you're here. Companionship is a normal part of life and you are entitled to once again seek that companionship. If it has been, at minimum, one year since your husband's death and you do not yet feel that you are making significant progress on your healing journey, if you feel "stuck" in your grief but that you just don't know how to move forward, please seek help!

---

### FROM THE STILETTO FILE

Just because you are no longer a teenager does NOT mean that all of the basic rules of dating safety go out of the window. PLEASE take care to remember:

- On the first date, and perhaps even for the first few meetings, **always meet in a public place**—a restaurant or coffeehouse are excellent locales. Do not go to his home, nor should you have him into your home…not yet.

- **Always keep your car with you**—no meeting someplace, parking your car and getting into his car to go somewhere else. I have had to do everything from beat a hasty retreat from a nightmare date to get home quickly due to emergencies and if any of these happens, you will need your car with you! Not only that, think about getting into a car with a virtual stranger. Enough said.

- **Be sure to let someone know where you're going to be and with whom**. You can write this information down for a babysitter or for your children if they are old enough to be left on their own. My daughter and I also **check in with one another throughout the day or evening**, regardless of whether or not she is at home; just so that whomever I'm out with knows that somebody somewhere is acutely aware of my whereabouts and/or is expecting my arrival at some point.

- **Guard your alcohol consumption carefully**. Aside from all of the drinking and driving caveats that we all observe, alcohol also lowers inhibition and good sense. Also, in this day and age, it's a fact that we have to guard against potential situations that simply did not exist twenty or thirty years ago. To that end, **never leave your drink unattended**, whether to hit the dance floor or use the restroom, and **accept a drink only from a bartender or other establishment employee—never from a stranger, no matter how nice he seems**.
- **Keep your cell phone charged and your gas tank full—at all times!**

### Chapter 11

# FIRST LOVE...

**(Or Plugging Holes?)**

Trust me when I tell you, your husband did NOT want you to spend the rest of your life alone, in pain and in mourning. That's not why you're here. You are meant to continue living and loving and given your open mind and spirit and open heart, you will meet someone wonderful and feel those incredible stirrings: the stirrings of love.

But how do you know it's truly love? How does anyone ever know if it's love? Sounds like either stupid questions or potential song titles and I know that you're hardly an adolescent. Still, this is your life we're talking about and the questions need to be asked. Why? It's because of our inherent nature as human beings to "plug holes".

You see a pothole in the street and you drive carefully around instead of going through it. You put a hole in your pantyhose with your brand new French manicure and you scurry to paint clear nail polish over it until the pantyhose hose can be replaced and you are using foul language all the while. Holes in teeth are painful and we rush to get them filled. Just as inconvenient, irritating or downright painful are the "holes" in life. We are conditioned to plug holes wherever we experience them and the same is true here.

The death of your husband has left a huge, gaping hole at the dinner table, in the easy chair, on the dance floor, in your bed next to you, in your heart and in the hearts of your children. The first instinct is to immediately plug that hole—more than likely, with a man. Plugging holes is a natural instinct and is even more likely to happen in a situation where the death may have been sudden. When that hole is plugged, when that gaping void is filled, the pain will stop, right?

Wrong.

It is completely unfair to you, your children and certainly to any new man in your life to simply "plug" this hole with another human being in an attempt to sidestep the "firsts" or your grief or the very real and understandable fear of being alone. You know by now that we do not make clear, reasonable and sensible decisions while in the midst of one of the most intense kinds of grief that one will ever experience. Before you can confidently decide and ultimately declare that you are truly in love with a new man, you must *rationally* consider these questions:

## 1. How much time has passed since the death?

You answered this question in The Dating Game, but it needs to be asked again. Why? It takes time to get to know someone and if your husband's death is recent (i.e., less than one year), you have scarcely had time to recover from that event and the natural emotional fallout, let alone get to know someone well enough to declare that it's love.

When I hear stories of a woman who found a new love or a new husband "in the middle of my grief" or exclaim excitedly that "he came along at the worst time of my life," I inwardly groan. The height of grief or the worst time in your life is *not* the time to introduce a new person into your life and into your heart. Like it or not, you *must* first recover from the death of your husband and you cannot accomplish that in a "microwave oven, two-and-a-half-minute-music-video, fast-food, hurry-up" fashion. You MUST take time!

## 2. Am I happy all by myself, on my own?

Being happy by yourself means a contentment to be in your home by yourself (with or without your children) and that you have a life that is your own and is fulfilling in its own right. By definition, your "fulfilling life" should not merely consist of running your children from activity to activity, baking cupcakes for the class parties, running the scout troop or heading up the PTA. Those are satisfying activities, true; however, you must have a life *apart* from your children. Your children are going to one day grow up and go away; that's what they are supposed to do. If you rely solely on your children or their activities to fulfill your life, you have placed an unfair burden on them and come the day that your children leave home—and they will—what then?

Do you have your own career, your own hobbies, your own pursuits, your own set of girlfriends with whom you lunch, drink or dine? You've likely had to backburner some, if not all of these things and now is the time to make your return! This is a time of discovering you; getting to know this curious, exciting new woman moving into a new life. Take the time to make that discovery.

## 3. Am I capable of going out *by myself* and having a good time?

I readily and happily admit that I am a people person. I love people. All people. I love meeting new people; I love the people whom I've known forever. I love going places with people; I love entertaining and having people into my home. Once a cheerleader *always* a cheerleader (yes, it's true and yes, I still have my uniform and my megaphone).

I *am* the dreaded People Person.

If it is difficult to go out alone as a woman, it is twice as difficult for the People Person, who is used to and in fact, in love with being surrounded by a crowd. Yet I knew that the only way that I could truly move forward and eventually open up my heart to another male presence in my life for all of the right reasons was to make absolutely sure that I could go out and enjoy myself…*all by myself*.

What a terrifying thought.

As with everything else on the healing journey, this too is a "baby-step" situation. I started venturing out by myself in small ways—lunch at a coffee shop with a newspaper; coffee at a coffeehouse with a book. When I felt stronger and more confident (which comes with time and "practice"), I "graduated" to going to movies and comedy clubs by myself—without books or newspapers. Later still, I started going to concerts, plays and fine dining establishments at night by myself.

That last one was so exciting; I actually called my mother after dinner to share the fact that I had dined at a five-star restaurant all by myself and was not taken pity upon or otherwise made to feel uncomfortable or conspicuous. In general, I didn't vaporize.

My biggest personal challenge that I issued to myself took place almost two years after Mike's death, after a business conference that I was attending in Las Vegas. Rather than leave immediately after the conclusion of the conference, I intentionally stayed in Las Vegas one extra day and night. I dined, gambled, meandered through shops (contributing heavily to the economy) and enjoyed my favorite city in the world *all by myself.*

It felt rather like the first day of kindergarten, except with champagne and slot machines.

When I returned home, I knew then that because I was able to go out by myself and genuinely enjoy myself without a man or my daughter or any kind of "distraction", that when the time came to introduce someone into my life, it would be because I would be legitimately ready for a companion; not because of a glaring void that needed to be filled.

## JUST FOR YOU

Have you been out to dinner by yourself? How about a movie, a play, an art gallery, a concert or a comedy club? I know that as women, we are accustomed to either traveling in packs or with a man; however, you must be happy and content with your own company before you can seriously involve someone in your life. Aside from which, this is the millennium; hotels, maitre d's, ushers and hosts of every sort bend over backwards to take care of a woman who is dining on her own or attending an event by herself—no more getting seated "in the back by the kitchen" for us! Hotels take particular care of women traveling by themselves and, in fact, many major hotels are now instituting "women only" floors to further ensure our safety.

I intentionally spent the first year after Mike's death focusing only on regaining my own health (which had suffered tremendously during and immediately after Mike's illness), spending time with my daughter and growing my business. I very deliberately did not date. Taking into consideration my People Person personality, I also recognized my own obvious inclination to plug holes. I did not want to simply "meet someone" in order to avoid the pain of the firsts—*any* of the firsts. Remember, when one is grieving, one does not make the most smart, rational choices, especially if the goal is simply to plug a hole.

I have coached many widows who have unwittingly found themselves in new relationships for which they were not yet ready for the simple reason that rather than risk being lonely or having to actually face and cope with their grief, they thought that it would be easier to simply "fill the emptiness" with another human being. Too late, they realized that what they instead succeeded in doing was *postponing* the inevitable—the grief, the pain and the adjustment to widowhood that we *all* have had to make. The problem is that now there is involved a very baffled and confused man who wants only to please his lady. The pity is that the harder he tries to do so, the more he will fail—and it's no one's fault!

Let's try to avoid that scenario by once again checking in with your head and your heart. The following quiz is for those of you who are involved with a potential "Someone Special".

## LOVING, LONGING... OR JUST PLAIN LONELY?

How do you know whether or not you are really in love? While there are certainly no "right" answers to this very complex question, there are definitely questions that you can consider which will help you determine whether or not you may be in love, whether you are *ready* to be in love or if, in fact, you are simply "plugging" those holes that we've talked about.

Take the following quiz and mark the answers that best apply to your current situation; remember, honesty isn't just the best policy—it's the only policy!

**1. It has been at least one year since my husband died.**
- True
- False

**2. Understanding that regardless of marital status, everyone experiences moments of loneliness, I am now generally happy and content on my own. I also have my own career and/or hobbies, friends, etc., independent of my children and/or their activities.**
- True
- False

**3. I have gone out by myself (to a movie, restaurant or other public place) and had a good time—without feeling lonely, self-conscious, conspicuous or otherwise completely uncomfortable—and I have done so more than once.**
- True
- False

**4. I generally do not mind being at home alone; even at nighttime.**
- True
- False

**5. Since the death of my husband, I have dated more than one man.**
- True
- False

I encourage you to go back over each one of these questions. When you can sincerely answer at least three of these questions as "true" (and be honest with yourself!) and all indicators point to a happy, contented, confident-in-her-own skin woman, you are likely in the frame of mind and heart to let yourself love in every sense of the word. If not, perhaps you aren't quite "there yet", which is fine—but you must also reassess whether you are feeling "in love" or "in need". There's a huge difference between the two. Your general feeling should be, "I need him because I love him"; rather than, "I love him because I need him".

## First Intimate Experience

You may be reading this thinking, *I do not believe in sex prior to or without the benefit of marriage.* You may be reading this having no problem whatsoever being physically intimate with someone to whom you are not married. Regardless of the category into which you fall, the moment is going to arrive. You will be taking one of the biggest "first steps" (if not the biggest first step) since your husband's death. It's huge, it's exciting, it's highly anticipated and it's terrifying.

Remarriage or not, you will arrive at the point in your life where you are moving forward into a physical relationship. Keeping your very best interests and feelings in mind, I am hoping that this decision has been made rationally and with much thought, discussion and care on everyone's part. In other words, this particular "first" should not be taking place after a Girls Night Out martini-fest at Club Of-The-Moment.

Not unlike the first date, you may again experience the "cheating twinge" discussed earlier. Irrespective of how long your husband has been gone, you may still feel as though you are cheating on him and if you're not cheating on him, then you're cheating on your children, for your late husband was their father and *what* would your children think?

Yes, the decision to become sexually active again can be a frightening one. From an emotional standpoint, your husband may have been the only man with whom you have ever been intimate. This is especially true of the young widow and the younger you are, the more likely that this may be the case. Even when you are seriously, deeply and passionately involved with someone new and you feel oh-so-ready, the decision to become intimate after being with only one man for your entire adult life is a daunting one.

From a practical standpoint, let's be honest, it's become a scary world out there. From mood-altering "date rape" drugs that can be slipped into drinks to the myriad of STD's that have been discovered in the last twenty-five years (many of which are incurable, one of which is fatal and many more of which can render you anything from miserable at best to infertile at worst), how many times have we been warned—by our physicians, dozens of women's magazines and afternoon talk shows—that "even if you know someone, you don't really 'know' them"?

Regardless of however many or however few men you may have been intimate with in your lifetime, trust me when I say that you will never more keenly aware of your physical flaws (real or imagined) than right at this moment in your new life. How *ever* will you be able to let anyone else see you with no makeup, stretch marks, puffy eyes or not-so-perfect thighs, when perhaps the only thing that stands up perkily on your body are the flyways in your hair?

Tell the truth—all of this kind of makes you want to limit your bedtime partner to microwave popcorn (which happens to go great with late night TV).

Nah, just kidding.

My first intimate experience after Mike's death took place two years later and was with my First Love. I was smart enough to wait until I was with a man with whom I was involved exclusively and with whom I was absolutely certain that I was in love. He was extremely sensitive to my situation and knew that he was both my "first love" since becoming widowed as well as my first physical involvement. To say that he was patient with me until the time was right would be an understatement and in fact, his consideration and respect for me and for our relationship was such that he was prepared to wait much longer.

Like you, and like any woman on this planet, I had concerns. These concerns started with, "I wonder if I even remember how to do this", ended with, "How am I going to hide all of the body flaws simultaneously" and in between, wondering if the lingerie store sold camouflage. After all, at the time, I was in my early forties, not my twenties and, childbirth notwithstanding, things don't quite "stand up" like they used to do.

I have great news for you:

---

## Men Don't Care!

---

As women, generally, and thanks in large part to the barrage of "ideal" (and completely unattainable) images in all forms of media to which we are exposed from about ten minutes after birth, we have become so consumed with our thighs and our hips and our tummies and our non-gravity-defying boobs and whether those boobs are "too big" or "too small" or point up or point down and whether or not we've shaved our legs (or anything else, come to that) or waxed (and I am not a fan of pouring hot wax on my nether regions) or the mere fact that we might not look like the next cover candidate for the *Sports Illustrated* swimsuit edition, that we are forgetting how to just plain *relax and enjoy ourselves*! Men—thank God—are simply not that concerned with any of it! Although everyone likes their packages wrapped prettily (and admit it ladies, that includes us, too!) and as cliché as this may sound, it really *is* what is on the inside that counts. Ask any man you know what the sexiest thing about a woman is and he will most likely list "confidence" at number one or, at the very least, in the Top Three (along with smile and sense of humor). I can assure you that your thighs or hips will be nowhere on his list.

I both teach and firmly believe that what you focus on, you will gravitate toward. If **you** are confident with **you** (flaws and all) and you are confident in the person with whom you are involved, your first (and subsequent) intimate experiences will be the loving, giving, wonderfully caring experiences that they should be and that you deserve.

Upon reaching this "milestone" in your relationship, an understanding and compassionate partner who knows you and your particular situation well and is more concerned about you and your needs, rather than his own needs, will in and of itself ease this most important transition in your life.

## CRY AND CARRY ON

Many women have asked me if I thought about my husband before or while I was intimate with my new love the first time and/or if I felt sad after the first time. This is not an uncommon or unreasonable question; yet my honest answer is no.

My personal timeline and specific timing for that moment in my life was perfect...for me. However, had I experienced any such sadness or regret, I know that without doubt or question, my First Love would have fully understood and even encouraged me to take a "step back".

My advice to you is if you find yourself feeling uncomfortable or sad or even depressed because you might have taken this step just a bit too soon, you must communicate this to your partner gently and honestly. Don't make him play the "What's Wrong/Nothing" game and you know the one that I'm talking about:

---

### WELCOME TO THE "WHAT'S WRONG / NOTHING" GAME
#### (Cue requisite cheesy game show music....)

Him: "Honey, you're so quiet. What's wrong?"

You: "Nothing. I'm fine."

Him: "Are you sure?"

You: (heavy sigh) "Yes, I'm fine."

Him: "You don't seem fine to me. Are you sure you're really all right?"

You: (still heavily sighing) "Yes, I'm totally fine. Quit asking me."

Him: "OK, if you're absolutely sure. Where do you want to go for dinner?"

You: (bursting into tears) "AAAAAAAAAHHHHHHHHHHH-HHH!!!!! You don't care about MEEEEEEEEE!!!!!!"

---

And so forth.

Explain to him honestly what's going on and what you're feeling. Any man who is worthwhile and worthy of you will sympathize and understand. He will also give you the time that you need to adjust to this new phase of your relationship—even if it means temporarily "suspending" the physical aspect for a while, until you are ready to try again. If he does not understand or is ridiculing, condescending, belittling or insensitive in any way, this is not the person for you. Do not walk, RUN out the front door and do not look back.

And what about those "cheating twinges"? They will subside and disappear, as well they should. You are not cheating on anyone—not your children, not your late husband and certainly not on the memory of your late husband. You are moving forward into a new life. Without casting any aspersions on your former life, that chapter of your life has ended. Just look at the new chapters that you are writing! Stop for a moment and just look at how far you've come on your healing journey!

---

### FROM THE STILETTO FILE

The same rules that we teach our children about safe sex apply to you as well. If your choice is to be sexually active, your partner MUST use a condom. This is non-negotiable. Any man who refuses to respect this all-important rule gets shown the door. If you are worried about "spoiling the mood" or are embarrassed to discuss the health, safety and well-being of the two of you, you should not be there in the first place. If you are firmly established as a monogamous couple (which I personally do advocate), but one or both of you have had multiple partners or had unprotected sex prior to your committing to each other, for your respective peace of mind, please get tested—for everything!

Just one more time: if you are truly having difficulty with this step in your life, I once again strongly encourage you to speak with your medical doctor, cleric or other professionals whom you trust and who can advise you wisely and compassionately. Life is meant for you to give and receive love in every aspect! Remember that if the going gets tough—the tough get help!

### Chapter 12

# "NOW YOU'LL HAVE CLOSURE"
## (And Other Myths Laid to Rest)

Baggage and closure are certainly two of the most overused words in our vernacular today.

Previously confined to airport luggage carousels, "baggage" has now become the "catch-all" word that is used to describe the life drama(s) of anyone who has had any kind of significant emotional event in his or her life. Also, sometimes used as a synonym for children (generally those of a single parent), "baggage" is a term that needs to be clearly defined, put in its proper place (that would be back on the airport carousels) and never EVER used to describe children—not ever!

"Closure" refers to that elusive component that, apparently, we are all assumed to be seeking on this journey called widowhood. How many times have you been told, "Now you'll have closure" (or words to that effect) since your husband's death? I'm guessing that you have heard this quite a lot; usually beginning about thirty minutes after the conclusion of the funeral service.

Let's examine these myths and misuses with the goal of laying both to rest, once and for all.

---

## Baggage—The Kind Without Wheels

Once used only as something to throw clothes into for transport, the word "baggage" has now become almost accusatory in nature. Remember in "The 'Firsts'—Part II (Definitely Not on the Calendar)", when, in referring to my status as a widow, a friend of mine told me that, "There's a lot of baggage there"? You'll recall that I took issue with the term "baggage" for two reasons: the first being that my late husband is not a suitcase.

I know that I said it once, but it bears repeating.

Second, and more importantly, simply because you have experienced and *survived* one of the most traumatic events of your lifetime, it does NOT mean that you are hauling baggage around.

Does this then mean that emotional "baggage" does not exist? Of course it does, but we need to *correctly* define exactly the meaning of the word. In its proper usage, "baggage" refers to events having triggered emotions of which one steadfastly refuses to just let go, inhibiting or eliminating altogether the ability to move forward.

---

Earlier, you met one of my dates, appropriately named, "I'm In My Late Forties And I Haven't Gotten Over My High School Sweetheart Who Dumped Me Decades Ago And Screwed Me Up For Life" Guy. Not only did he spend the majority of the evening waxing nostalgic about his high school sweetheart who unceremoniously dumped him in high school (shocking!), he also maintained that because of this landmark experience, he had since been unable to pursue a healthy relationship. While I'm sure you are giggling, I'm confident that you are also wondering what he was doing out on a date in the first place.

So was I.

Actually, what I was thinking at that moment was that we were both in our forties (which certainly allowed for ample recovery time from such a breakup); that just about everyone on the planet was dumped at least once in high school (including yours truly); that this must have been one amazing chick to have messed him up for the past thirty-odd years.

Another first date/last date combo was with a man who spent the entire evening complaining loudly—with the most colorful profanity, no less—about his ex-wife. This is not necessarily unusual until you consider that this one-sided conversation consumed the better part of three hours as well as the fact that he had been divorced for *over twenty years.*

This, my friend, is baggage! We've already discussed that emotional baggage becomes painful and troublesome when some of the things that have happened to you now cause you to hold onto the past. When you are stuck there, you cannot take the necessary steps to move forward from hurtful events to a place of healing and renewal. This is the "baggage" to which we need to be referring. It is otherwise unfair to state or assume that simply because a wife lost her husband, she is now carrying "baggage". We won't have it!

---

## WIDOWS WEAR STILETTOS LAUGH-O-METER

During another dating experience lasting approximately one hour—which was about fifty-five minutes too long for me—a different man inquired as to how my husband passed away; a common question and one which I never mind answering. I had just begun to answer his question in a very general and completely calm manner when he abruptly cut me off, literally *put his hands over his ears* and said, "I don't want to hear any more; that's 'baggage'."

No, I didn't dump my coffee in his lap, but I'll admit that I thought about it.

You see, this is *not* an example of "baggage". Had I been sitting there on a date, dissolving into tears over my husband's passing years after the fact, I would readily admit there might have been some emotional "baggage" that needed attending. However, that was not the case. This person decided that based **exclusively** on the fact that I was a widow and that there had been a dramatic and significant event in my life, this in and of itself equated "baggage".

Do not permit *anyone* to apply this moniker to you. Do not let anyone discredit your recovery in such a callous and uncaring manner. Your spirit is too strong and you have come way too far. While no one actively seeks the title of "widow", it is nonetheless a title that you should wear with pride and love. You loved someone deeply and were deeply loved in return. You were there until "the end". The love that you shared remained intact, unwavering and strong. I once again ask you, how many people in this day and age can lay claim to that?

One more vitally important and non-negotiable point: Anyone who refers to your children as "baggage" is not worth the time of day. Children are not baggage or burdens or inanimate objects that you are forced to "lug" around. Anyone who does not recognize this fact should not get the pleasure of your company. Ever. End of discussion.

P.S. I never spoke with any of the aforementioned men ever again!

## BAGGAGE "HANDLER" OR BAGGAGE BE-GONE?

Let's have a look at your experiences with the word "baggage" —how often have you heard the word regarding your situation? If you've actually been accused of having "baggage", first let's determine if you actually *are* carrying a bit of emotional baggage, we can help you begin to let go.

Mark the answers that best fit your **overall** experiences:

**1. As a widow, I have either myself used or had the word "baggage" used in regard to my situation.**
- Never
- Occasionally
- Quite a bit

2. If you answered "occasionally" or "quite a bit", why do you think that the word "baggage" is being used (either by you or others)? Think carefully—do you believe that it was simply because you are now widowed or might there be other factors involved?

_____

_____

_____

_____

3. Has anyone ever referred to your children as "baggage"?
- Yes
- No

4. If you answered "yes" to question 3, what steps, if any, did you take to correct the person or people who made this remark?

_____

_____

_____

_____

_____

5. Now that you've read about and understand that "baggage" refers to the refusal to let go of and move forward from hurtful events to a place of healing and renewal (and is *never* used in reference to children), do you believe yourself to be "carrying baggage"? Keep in mind that there is no right or wrong answer…it just has to be an *honest* answer!
- Yes, most definitely
- Perhaps a little bit, but I'm working on it
- No

6. If your answer to question 5 was in the affirmative, what factors lead you to believe that you might be dealing with "baggage" (i.e., widowed for over one year and still cannot speak about your husband without crying; feeling as though life has no meaning or purpose, etc.). Please

note: The outside opinions of Everyone Else are not to be taken into consideration here!

_____

_____

_____

_____

7. If, in fact, you feel like you are a "Baggage Handler", what steps are you willing to take to work toward dropping the "baggage" and moving into a place of peace? This might involve anything from seeking professional help to simply taking the time to confront, deal with and move forward from grief, if you have not already taken the time with yourself to do so.

_____

_____

_____

_____

_____

## Closure; In Pursuit of...

I'm going to save you a great deal of time and aggravation in the search for closure by divulging a huge secret:

There is no such thing as "closure". Quit looking for it. We need to file this along with other myths such as:

* **"Lose 30 pounds in 30 days."**
* **"If you keep making that face, it will freeze that way."**
* **"Linebacker-sized shoulder pads will make your waist look smaller."**

(Okay, that last myth admittedly died along with acid washed denim, Day-Glo bike pants, nighttime soap operas and that inimitable hairstyle known as The Mullet.)

If you are searching for closure, you are better off instead searching for the pot of gold at the end of the rainbow; you are hunting for something that simply does not exist.

"Closure", as defined by most, means that you have either the desire or the capability to put "it" behind you. "It" refers to the death of your husband and/or the events leading up to his death. In point of fact, many people expect "closure" in a "dust off your hands, 'glad that's over, now let's get on with life'" fashion. Essentially, "closure" has just become a diplomatic way of saying "get over it", because many people are quite uncomfortable with the concept of his death and your grieving.

Unimaginable.

The loss of your husband is a life-altering event that has shaken you to your core. Yet, after some time has passed, then, after significant time has passed, when this magical "closure" doesn't happen, you wonder if something is wrong with you. How is it possible that you cannot put this experience "behind" you? Why do you not have this mysterious "closure?"

Because you can't have something that isn't real.

There is not now, nor was there ever "closure"—or any escaping that fact. The experience that was the loss of your husband remains with you always. It is something that you carry with you every day. It is impossible to "close" it. The experience becomes a component of you, just like a body part. I invite you to embrace this experience called widowhood and make it a part of you. You are forever transformed as a result of this journey. Why would you want to slam a door on that? Do you want to leave the horrible feeling of daily grief and anguish behind? Most definitely. Close the door on your past? Don't even try!

Depending on where you are in your journey, your emotions differ at first: it feels like you cry incessantly, you can't even mention your husband's name without bursting into tears and your days consist of "going through the motions" of life. As time passes, you begin moving slowly and, hopefully, steadily through your healing journey. The overwhelming part of the grief lessens and, gradually, a feeling of normalcy—even joy and laughter—returns to your life.

Rather than think of your journey in terms of achieving "closure", I invite you to think of this as a life-altering event from which you **move forward**. Instead of slamming some imaginary door on your past in the name of "closure", you *embrace* the past; it has become a *part* of you and now you are moving forward from it, into a new life.

It is my fervent belief that those who are seeking closure are potentially setting themselves up for additional pain. You expect that one day you will wake up and suddenly, the sadness isn't with you anymore, and you anxiously look forward to that day. As the days turn into weeks and months, and you discover that this doesn't happen, you begin to wonder when you'll ever experience this closure that everyone expects to wash over you. As time continues on, the overwhelming sorrow no longer rule your days and nights as it once seemed, but the pain, the void, the yearning for "just five more minutes" with your husband doesn't go away. It diminishes, it takes its proper place in your heart and its necessary perspective in your daily life—but it will never completely disappear. What is the end result? You begin to believe that something is wrong with you because you haven't experienced "closure"—and nothing could be farther from the truth.

My husband has been gone for years now and I have experienced much in the years since his passing. A pre-adolescent when her daddy died, our daughter Kendall is now a young adult. I have changed homes and changed careers; dated and subsequently fell in love, then fell back out of love and moved forward from *that* experience; took a significant amount of time "off" from the dating/love arenas; changed my hairstyle I don't know *how* many times; rediscovered dating and fell in love *again*. It has been and continues to be an incredible and amazing personal journey.

Yet, seldom does a day pass that I don't want to have that "five minutes" with my late husband—to share a triumph, to relate a challenge, to laugh out loud with him, to catch him up on what Kendall is doing— the list is endless. However, as is essential and as I know was his wish, I have moved forward from his death as well as the over-two-year-period of his illness that led to his passing.

Would it be accurate to say that I've had "closure", that I've dusted off my hands as it were with an, "Okay, that's done, what's next" attitude? Absolutely not. I cannot and I will not "close" my mind or my heart to the experience that was being a loving wife in a wonderful marriage; nor would I choose to put that life on a shelf somewhere in my mind. Just as you must be warmed by the memories of your past with your husband, I, too, am proud of my past and the life that my husband and I shared.

On the other hand, should one live in or for the past?

No.

If you were content doing that, you wouldn't be reading this book. It is absolutely possible—and necessary—to honor, cherish and treasure the past without living in the past and we've discussed that in our journey together in this book. You clearly want to move ahead with your life and that's fantastic—but *please* don't continue in the quest for the mystical and completely elusive "closure". Instead, view your experience as a young widow as something that has become a part of your being; it's another new dimension to the person that you truly are. It is knowledge and understanding that has strengthened you in many ways. It's an awareness and an acceptance of the woman you are becoming and believe me, *that* you will never want to "close"!

I want you to read and then wholeheartedly commit to the following promise. Be sure to review this promise *every single time* you hear the word "closure"…and then smile!

---

## MY PROMISE TO ME

- I recognize that the "closure" that I expected to have and/or Everyone Else expects me to have **does not exist**—it is a myth.

- I accept the fact that I am always going to want to have "five more minutes" with my husband that I'm not going to have. However, this does not mean that I am living in or for the past; nor does it mean that I am not moving forward with my life in a positive way.

- I will endeavor to make the experience of widowhood something from which I **move forward**, rather than something that I feel compelled to try to "close" or "forget" or otherwise attempt to ignore.

- I realize that not only is it impossible for me to "close" the door on my past that was being a loving wife to my late husband, I neither have to, nor do I wish to.

- I acknowledge that I can honor and pay homage to my late husband and the memories that I am free to openly treasure, while at the same time continuing to move forward on my healing journey. Further, though I will hold precious the corner of my heart that will always belong to my husband, this in no way means that I am incapable of loving once again, once my "healing timeline" tells me that I'm ready to do so.

- I will take great pride in myself for the positive way that I am facing my future. With each passing day, I am becoming stronger, more confident and more peaceful and content as I transition into my new life filled with hope and promise.

### Chapter 13

# B-U-L-L OR Y-E-E-H-A-H
**(The Choice is Yours)**

Regardless of how much or how little time has passed since your husband's death, when you make that decision to venture out into the world once more, in whatever form that venturing out takes place, people around you will have an opinion.

Whether it's a decision to change jobs, change homes, change hairstyles, begin dating again or, in general, start taking steps forward into a new life, you will hear opinions and you will hear those opinions everywhere: at work, at school, at coffee with the other moms, at the gym, on your child's playing field, at church or temple—the list goes on and on. You will wonder what people talked about before you were around to discuss. Worse yet, some of these people might even include members of your family, members of your husband's family or people whom you once considered friends. Insensitive individuals will have no problem nor even pause for a moment before letting you know what they think, despite the hurt that they might cause you. So what do you do?

*Exactly what you damn well please.* Now hang in there with me on this.

When I was thirteen years old, my mother gave me an adorable little plaque to hang in my very nineteen seventies-decorated bedroom. It was framed in lime green, hot pink and orange and it read simply:

> "Be concerned with
> what you must do;
> Not what the people think."
> [Anonymous]

These are some of the wisest words ever written and throughout my life, I have tried with all of my being to live by those words.

And I have been largely unsuccessful.

Make no mistake, I am a strong person. I am both an outgoing and outspoken person. I am an independent and self-sufficient person. I am also a person who has always desperately needed the approval of everyone with whom I have ever come into contact.

All right, that last line may have been a slight exaggeration, but the fact is that other people's opinions have always mattered to me. The thought of any person or group of people not approving of my words or my actions was unthinkable to me. I am—in every sense of the phrase—a "people pleaser".

And then…

Fully two *years* after Mike's death, I met my "First Love", whom you met in The "Firsts"—Part II. At that point, in my mind, I had done everything "right" in the ways of widowhood. I had spent the necessary time alone discovering myself to ensure that I wasn't plugging the holes that we've talked about; I resumed dating when the time was appropriate for me to do so and had dated a variety of men prior to my "First Love". I was continuing to help Kendall in her recovery from losing her daddy; I spent time focused on my business, which was by then flourishing once again. I was ready for a new love to enter into my life and my new love was ready for me. It was awesome. I was over-the-moon, super-sappy greeting card, walking into walls, bats-in-the-stomach, goofy-eyed, happier-than-I-had-been-in-longer-than-I-could-remember in *LOVE*.

Then we "went public".

True, there were many people who were happy for us, including Kendall, our respective families and our closest friends. However, much to my stunned surprise, the uninvited "cousin" of our old friend "Everyone Else" showed up at the party. We'll refer to this uninvited cousin as, "Those People".

---

## ...AND JUST WHO EXACTLY ARE "THOSE PEOPLE"?

I was astounded to discover that Those People were not quite as well-meaning as Everyone Else, who was there when I was in the heaviest period of my grief and was at least trying to be helpful.

As opposed to Everyone Else, Those People apparently expected me to be "The Perpetual Widow": shroud myself in black, build shrines devoted to my late husband and weep for the rest of my life. Instead of being loving, kind and supportive, Those People were saying that I had no respect for my husband's memory. Those People were relieved that I wasn't "prowling" after their husbands—because according to Those People, that's how young widows supposedly behave. Those People wondered out loud what kind of example I was setting for my child. In point of fact, and lacking the nerve (or sense) to ask the adults, Those People had the audacity to actually **question my then thirteen-year-old child** as to the status of my love life. Those People even went so far as to say that I was "dancing on [my] husband's grave."

Even worse was that I later discovered that Those People were not about to limit their opinions, attacks, "musings and mulling" to the state of my love life. Those People were also going to comment on and criticize everything from my physical appearance to my daughter's choices in handbags—yes, Those People have no problem going after children as well.

Ever get the feeling that you were back in high school, only you don't remember getting into the Way Back Machine and Sherman and Mr. Peabody are nowhere around?

First, for any normal, rational woman who has reached the milestone of embarking on a new relationship subsequent to her husband's death, the "point-and-stare" chatter and treatment would be difficult to comprehend. To the People Pleaser, it is poison. It is absolutely toxic.

As you can well imagine, I was devastated.

I was hurt beyond measure, because I fervently believed that I had done everything "right". Why weren't Those People happy for me? I was quite confident that enough time had passed since Mike's death; it surely felt like enough time had passed. I was conducting myself in a manner befitting my position in life. After all, I was in my early forties; surely I was entitled to love another and be loved in return once more. Certainly I was not expected to wear black and mourn the loss of my husband for the rest of my days. How could Those People say such horrific things, especially when no one was saying anything derogatory to or about my new man?

Suddenly, I was reminded of the whole 1950s-era mindset when, if you were a sexually active guy, you were a "stud" and you were "cool"; but if you were the girl he was getting busy with, you were a "bad girl" and a "slut". Someone please explain this logic to me.

Several years after Mike's death, I decided to dedicate my life to the emotional support, education and recovery of millions of women exactly like us—those who became widowed far too early in life. With that decision, *Widows Wear Stilettos* was born. This decision was not made because I was somehow starved for recognition or some supposed "limelight"; rather, the decision was made because I knew that there were millions in need and, as you are well aware, there was little or no support available.

So I went to work.

I retired from a lucrative career. I took many months to build a "team" of fantastic experts and professionals whose daily help augments the messages of healing and hope offered to those who needed it—and they continue to do so, even on an international level. Our website, **www. widowswearstilettos.com**, was later introduced and it is an interactive website that helps tens of thousands in need. I spent a long time writing the book you are currently holding in your hands. We produced a CD

(*Widows Wear Stilettos…What Now?*) so that those in need could get help immediately, both soon after becoming widowed and later on in their healing journey.

Many of the widowed from all over the world were finally getting help, receiving education and emotional support and even becoming friends with one another through the website—exchanging emails, letters, recipes, children's pictures and holiday cards. To our collective delight, the media then took interest in our cause and couldn't wait to tell our story; resulting in reaching even more women (and men) in need. Television and radio came calling, as did magazines, newspapers and web media. My "hometown" newspaper picked up the story of *Widows Wear Stilettos*, how we came into existence and the work to which we are dedicated. We were then informed that the story was considered to be important enough to run on the front page of the newspaper.

THE FRONT PAGE!

To all of us, this moment in time was huge. We were all so ecstatic— imagine how many more people would learn about *Widows Wear Stilettos* and would find the help for which they were searching so desperately.

Until…

The article came out and almost immediately, responses started pouring in—but not the responses that you would expect. These instead were responses written by, you guessed it:

## Those People.

Unlike the thousands of beautiful letters that I receive each month through **www.widowswearstilettos.com** that express thanks and gratitude for having found *Widows Wear Stilettos*, we were instead victims of some of the most hateful and spite-filled comments that I've ever seen: comments attacking everything from my hair, makeup and fashion choices (not exactly what you would call paramount in importance) to our alleged "ulterior motives" with *Widows Wear Stilettos*. Most remarkable was the fact that <u>none of these derogatory comments was written by a widow!</u>

Yet once again, and as I was before when "going public" with my

First Love, I was devastated. I was almost overwhelmed by the hurt. All I wanted to do was help people and I retired from the aforementioned lucrative job (complete with a lucrative salary) to do so. All I truly cared about was educating those who needed and wanted so badly to learn how to live an abundant life after losing a husband and couldn't find the tools to do it. To then again have to endure such pettiness, incredible insensitivity and lack of compassion—except this time, in a very public forum—it was almost too much to bear.

Then finally, at long last…

**I GOT ANGRY.**

(Okay, so it took me awhile…)

However, I was not angry with Those People, as you might reasonably expect. While admittedly, Those People are not exactly on my holiday greeting card list, my anger was directed instead toward myself. I was angry with myself for even *caring* what Those People were saying. I had always believed myself to be just a little more sophisticated and intelligent than the likes of Those People – why was I now permitting myself to worry over gossip and the opinions and the pettiness and the lack of compassion?

Then out of the blue and over thirty years after I had first received it, the words on that wonderful little plaque that my mother had given me so long ago came echoing back in my ears:

---

"Be concerned with
what you must do;
Not what the people think."
[Anonymous]

---

And that's when my attitude began to change.

I began to chant the same thing over and over to myself: **B**eyond **U**nderstanding = **L**ittle **L**ives (or "**B-U-L-L**" for short). Who *are* Those People to me? Certainly not people who have my best interests or concerns at heart. Rather, Those People are completely **B**eyond **U**nderstanding with tiny **L**ittle **L**ives, who really have nothing better to focus on than what is going on in the lives of others. Why continue to lend attention or power or any energy whatsoever to **B-U-L-L**!

---

### WIDOWS WEAR STILETTOS LAUGH-O-METER

Bobby Slayton, a well-known and absolutely brilliant comedian and actor who played Joey Bishop in HBO's biopic about the Rat Pack and co-starred in the Barry Levinson comedy *Bandits* alongside Bruce Willis and Billy Bob Thornton, is not only a very important person in our family, but is indeed also a wonderful positive role model and "uncle" to Kendall. A few years ago, I was talking to him about a less-than-marvelous stay that I had experienced at a five-star hotel. When he asked me if I had taken up my various complaints with the hotel management, I told him no; I didn't want to be perceived as being bitchy or difficult (by a bunch of *strangers*, no less).

He then looked at me with an expression of astonishment (or disgust; I'm not sure which) and after muttering an unprintable comment about my supposed bitchiness, then asked, "Do you realize how stupid you sound?"

I said that he was a brilliant comedian. A diplomat he is not.

After I finished laughing hysterically, he then went on to ask, "How long are you going to worry about what other people think about you? So **what** if people think you're bitchy! You are **not** going to be everybody's friend. Not **everyone** is going to love you—that's just the way it is. And besides, you might get a free stay from the hotel!"

At least he had his priorities straight.

---

What our sweet friend could not have realized at the time is that our conversation, humorous as it sounds, actually succeeded in helping me to overcome some forty-odd years of people-pleasing behavior.

Even though the conversation was quite funny at the time, I thought carefully about the wisdom behind the conversation for several days afterward. Who *was* I trying to please? Whose approval is important? And what *are* the "consequences" if someone—Those People, for instance—don't happen to approve of who I am or what I have to say or how I look or what I wear or how I raise my child or what I'm about or how I generally live my life?

I do again acknowledge that these may be somewhat controversial observations and at first blush, insensitive observations as well. It might sound as though I'm advising you to go about your life without caring about the feelings of others and that's not it at all. However, I have also learned the hard way that if you are determined to live your life according to opinion poll, you will ultimately please no one, including you. This is your new life that we're talking about and it's a life that you have earned the right to live how you see fit, in peace and in abundance.

P.S.: By the way, Bobby was right—I did get a free hotel stay and guess what? Not once did anyone cast aspersions, either on my complaints or on my personality.

(Well, at least not to my face.)

## Energy Givers vs. Energy Drainers

I have long taught that every single person on the entire planet can be categorized into one of two columns: Energy Givers and Energy Drainers.

Energy Givers are fantastic. They are the people who bring a smile to your face; those who buoy your spirits and for whom you are better (or at least *feel* better) for having spent time in their spaces. They are enthusiastic, positive and uplifting; they are, in fact, as contagious as the chicken pox in a day care center in the springtime.

It doesn't mean that Energy Givers don't have bad days or problems and challenges of their own; it's just that they choose not to burden you with them or lend additional power to negativity, other than whatever power they need to resolve the challenges as quickly as possible. Remarkably, most of the Energy Givers whom I am blessed enough to have in my life have had seemingly insurmountable obstacles to overcome and not once will you ever hear an Energy Giver complain or whine about his or her lot in life.

To the contrary, Energy Drainers are just that—draining. Spend enough time with an Energy Drainer and you'll feel like someone just let all of the air out of your tires. When you ask Energy Drainers how they are, they'll tell you, in detail and it's never good—their job stinks, they're full of aches and pains and ailments ALL of the time, the dog has fleas, the oven door is broken, they are *always* tired. They are the living example of the cartoon character with the perpetual rain cloud over his head. An Energy Drainer's glass isn't simply half-empty—the glass has a lipstick stain, a cigarette butt floating in the bottom and it's probably full of dribble holes anyway—just ask them. To an Energy Drainer, it's almost unbearable to see someone who is happy, content and fulfilled.

Being around an Energy Drainer will leave you completely bereft of vigor, of ambition and perhaps with a complete lack of faith in yourself — or in humanity, come to that! Misery doesn't just love company; misery loves a great big crowd and they want to make you a lifetime member of the club. Their "get-up-and-go" went ahead and "got up and went" a long time ago. I promise you that without exception, Those People, every single one of them, whomever they may be, are also Energy Drainers and they will suck you dry.

## GET AWAY FROM THEM!

You see, you will never find an Energy Giver among Those People. Energy Givers are too busy leading their lives and being happy and content within themselves. They are also certain to be thrilled for you and the fact that you have rediscovered love or changed careers or sold your home or switched your hairstyle or got a fabulous new wardrobe after what you have had to endure. As opposed to Those People, who are **B**eyond **U**nderstanding with **L**ittle **L**ives (**B-U-L-L**), Energy Givers are **Y**our **E**xcited, **E**nthusiastic **H**appy **A**nd **H**ooray-for-you circle of love or what we'll call **Y-E-E-H-A-H**.

Funny how that works, isn't it?

Sometimes it's not so easy getting yourself away from Energy Drainers. You may work with them, you may live next door to them and you may even be related to them. If you cannot get away from them entirely, try to at least limit your time with them. When they swing into their Negative Dance (and they will) and try to dash anything from your dreams to your dinner plans, I encourage you to go back in your mind to your elementary school days and that old playground rhyme:

> "I am rubber,
> you are glue,
> Whatever you say
> bounces off of me
> and sticks to you!"

First and foremost, you will hear laughter in your head.

Secondly, and in other more mature words, the opinions of Those People, whom we now know to be the Energy Drainers of the world, *cannot and must not* influence you or otherwise give you cause for doubt, guilt or shame. Make the conscious choice to refuse to allow it. Put on a smile, rejoice in your new love or your new job or your new home in a new place and that you are now standing in the doorway of a new, exciting life. Then get yourself around Energy Givers—fast!

## FROM THE STILETTO FILE
### In-Laws or Outlaws?

What about your in-laws? They will certainly have an opinion as to how you lead your life, particularly if you have children with whom grandparents, aunts, uncles and cousins may want to continue a relationship. On some level, and though completely unfair to you, they may even feel a little bit betrayed as they watch you move forward into a new life.

(...and here come the "cheating twinges" again!)

Should this be the case, be sure to "handle with care"; after all, your husband's family has suffered a loss as well. Explain to them quietly, rationally and patiently that while you will always love your late husband, the time has come for you to continue forward, be it with a new man, a new career, a new home, a new city and/or a new state. Demonstrate your willingness to work with them—visits with the children if desired, perhaps your continued attendance at family gatherings with the understanding that this may eventually include a new man in your life.

It is up to you to make it very clear that this is your life that you are entitled to lead in the manner that you see fit. Any inappropriately personal questions, comments, unsolicited opinions or complaints are neither needed nor welcomed and will not be tolerated.

## JUST FOR YOU

Bottom line, guys: Those People are going to talk. Those People have the capacity to be insensitive, hurtful, petty and rude. That's it. It's out of your control. Remember, you are the young widow, the curiosity. Those People are the Energy Drainers, quite consumed with the business of being miserable and taking as many along for the ride as possible. They believe that since you're a young widow and because of your life's particular set of circumstances, you have misery "baked right in". Prove them wrong! Believe me, after Those People are finished talking about you, they will talk about something or someone else—most likely whoever isn't in the room at the moment.

Are you going to let Those People or the Energy Drainers of the world lead your life for you? Your answer needs to be a resolute and out loud NO. As long as you continue to see to the needs, health and welfare of your children, you answer to **you**. Period. If you have met someone wonderful and he is fifteen years younger than you are or twenty years older than you are; if you've decided that now is the time in your life for your dream career (*whatever* that dream career is!); if you've decided to sell your house and all of your worldly possessions and go peddle bait in Bora Bora and live in a hut, then YOU DO IT!

You have paid some pretty incredible dues. You are walking a journey that most people will never walk and therefore will never truly understand. To put any weight on or invest any energy in negative opinions is nothing more than a waste of perfectly good energy as well as valuable time and life, as we widows well know, is simply too short.

Lastly and above all, I urge you to always remember:

> "Be concerned with
> what you must do;
> Not what the people think."
> [Anonymous]

**B-U-L-L** or **Y-E-E-H-A-H**. Which do you choose?

## WIDOWS WEAR STILETTOS "HEART MONITOR"

Let's now look at the Energy Givers and Energy Drainers in your life. This is going to help you not only stay focused on the positive people in your life, but also help you to refocus your own attitude toward the positive. Remember, honesty counts!

• Write down who you believe to be the five biggest Energy Givers in your life. By definition, Energy Givers are the people who are generally upbeat and positive; they bring a smile to your face and lift you up. You are better off for having spent time in their company.

_____

_____

_____

_____

_____

• What makes these people Energy Givers?

_____

_____

_____

_____

• Now, write down who you believe to be the five biggest Energy Drainers in your life. Remember, Energy Drainers are people who are generally negative. They may tend to be hypercritical (especially of others), pessimistic and may cause you to have an uncontrollable desire to run screaming from the room.

_____

_____

_____

_____

_____

•      What makes these people Energy Drainers?

_____

_____

_____

_____

_____

•      Now it's honesty time. Looking at yourself, **generally speaking** and widowhood notwithstanding, do you consider yourself to be an Energy Giver or an Energy Drainer?

_____

_____

_____

_____

_____

•      What makes you either an Energy Giver or an Energy Drainer?

_____

_____

_____

_____

•      If you feel that you are an Energy Drainer, what are some of the things that you can do to begin to refocus your attitude toward the positive?

_____

_____

_____

_____

_____

_____

• Since becoming widowed and to your knowledge, have you been the victim of gossip, opinions, conjecture or otherwise hurtful or malicious activity?

_____

_____

_____

_____

_____

• If so, by whom and what was said?

_____

_____

_____

_____

• How did it make you feel? Did you confront the situation at the time? Is it a situation that is ongoing?

_____

_____

_____

_____

• What immediate steps can you take in order to put yourself around the Energy Givers on your list on a regular basis?

_____

_____

_____

_____

_____

## MY PROMISE TO ME

- I understand that most people have Energy Givers and Energy Drainers in their lives. However, I also understand that it is vital to my healing journey to spend as much time around Energy Givers as is possible.
- I will spend as much time as possible with the Energy Givers on my list. I will further seek out other Energy Givers to add to that list.
- At the same time, I will limit my time spent with Energy Drainers to as little as is necessary. I will not permit *any* Energy Drainers to consume my spirit or otherwise deter me from moving ahead in a positive manner.
- Lastly, if I am right now an Energy Drainer myself, I will do *whatever* it takes to redirect my attitude and outlook toward the positive and promising future that awaits—and I now realize that all I have to do is *allow* that future to begin!

### Chapter 14

# TO REMARRY
# OR NOT TO REMARRY?
**(That Indeed is the Question!)**

The decision to marry your late husband was likely a pretty easy decision to make. Whether yours was a first or subsequent marriage; whether it was a "from scratch" family (you started out as just two and either stayed that way or welcomed children later on) or a "blended" family (either one or both of you brought children into the marriage), the "basics" were intact: you met, you fell in love, you got married, you celebrated and moved into a new life together.

This time, however, making the decision to marry is not quite as simple. Why?

For starters, neither you nor your late husband left your marriage willingly. This was not a situation of divorce where one person left another intentionally and with forethought—where there might likely have been at least a little bit of animosity involved. On the contrary, yours was a marriage where you were happy and thriving and the life you had together and/or as a family was rudely and sadly cut short. The question you ask yourself is: do you "pick up where you left off" when you're married to someone else?

Next, there is a very real, solid and practical fear of winding up a widow again. We already know that women generally outlive men; we're clearly proof of that! You have already gone through The Unimaginably Horrible Widow Journey once, which was one-too-many trips down that road, thank you.

What about your children? They've lost their daddy and no matter how great they may feel about your new love and the prospect of a new life as a new family, on some level, they may see you as trying to "replace" Dad. Ouch!

There is also the practical side. You may be receiving financial benefits as a widow that you may lose once you remarry. You must take this very important point into consideration; particularly if you already have children.

So you are now undoubtedly asking yourself, "Am I ready for this?" or perhaps, "Do I really need this?"

How I wish there was one simple answer for everyone. The fact is that when it comes to the question of remarriage, there is no one right answer for everyone. Understanding that, let's look at each of these factors and potential fear-makers to help you reach the best possible decision for you.

## The Last Marriage... Wasn't the "Last Marriage"!

The first feeling that you may be experiencing is complete surprise! Do you remember a time, not so long ago, when you could never in a million years even imagine yourself with another man? Now just look at you! Whatever your decision, the one thing above all that should be celebrated is the healing that you have experienced to this point.

Even with the celebration, though, you may be feeling conflicted. You still have love for your late husband—remember no one ended your marriage on purpose. So here you are, in love with two men at the same time, right?

Not exactly.

I have been widowed enough years to share this absolute certainty with you. The love that you have for your late husband never ever goes away. Not ever. Not with time, not with emotional "distance" from the death, not with selling your home and moving, not even with the introduction of new love into your life. As we learned earlier, the "corner" of your heart that belonged to your late husband will *always* belong to him and nothing and no one will ever change that. Your life with your late husband eventually becomes like a treasured photo album that you "revisit" over and over again. It is with much love, warmth and many smiles that you will look back upon and "revisit", if you will, that wonderful priceless album of your life with your late husband.

However, I must again gently and lovingly remind you that—he is gone. The chapter of your life that you shared with him has come to its end. You are young, there is much life left to be lived and love to share as well. It is absolutely possible for you to both treasure the love of and life with your late husband while being in love with and beginning a new life with the wonderful someone with whom you stand on the threshold of a brand new start.

## Once Was More Than Enough

As noted earlier, it is statistically proven, over and over again, that women outlive men. You have to then face the very real possibility that you could wind up a widow once again—and that's enough to scare anybody who's already been down this road!

But you know what? Were we to let fear of any sort govern and rule our lives, we would never get into our cars, get onto an airplane (which I fear, loathe and despise, but I fly anyway), go on a first date, try the blue eyeshadow instead of brown eyeshadow, buy the four-inch red pointy toe stilettos or let our children out of our sight, regardless of age.

While it's completely understandable that you fear being "back where you were" in the earlier stages of your healing journey and acknowledging that the fear of death—anyone's death—is the greatest fear of them all, you nonetheless cannot let this fear stand in the way of your future. Any more than you wouldn't stop your child from crossing the street for his entire life out of fear of him being hit by a car, you cannot let the fear of a repeat of the widow experience paralyze you.

I would like you instead to marvel at your strength, your vigor, your character, your integrity and the fact that you can proffer your new love the assurance that no matter how tough the road may get, when it comes to "for better or worse" or "in sickness and in health", you are an expert and that as you know you can lean on him, he in turn will be able to lean on you.

## JUST FOR YOU

Step out in faith, step out in love and step out in the understanding of just how incredible you are! Most people will never realize the true depths of their strengths and despite the immensely difficult obstacles that you've had to overcome, you *have* made such a discovery. What an amazing gift to have been able to discover just how strong you are!

---

### Your Children—
### The Past, Your Present and Everyone's Future

I have always chosen to include my daughter in decisions that would ultimately affect her life and I have always done so in an age-appropriate manner. I believe that it's unfair to go through life with an antiquated, "because I said so" attitude toward children and to make a decision to remarry absent your children's knowledge or input is unfair.

Upon hearing your news about remarriage, your children may be absolutely thrilled and run for the rice to throw at you. Your children may stare at you as if you have two heads. Your children may scream and cry and accuse you of forgetting their father and the "how could you's" will rain down on you like the rice you were hoping for instead. Even if they are excited for you and no matter how much they profess to love this new man in all of your lives, somewhere in the backs of their minds lurks the question, "Is Mommy replacing Daddy?"

---

The answer is an emphatic "NO".

Sit down with your child or children and discuss this very important step honestly. Though you may be disheartened if your children's reaction is anything other than sheer joy, you must nonetheless listen to your children with an open mind and an open heart. Be ready to receive and address all of their reactions in a calm and rationale manner. Do not get defensive or confrontational; you are the adult here. While being understanding of their love for and loyalty to Dad, be prepared to explain to them that while all of you will always love Daddy, it's also perfectly natural and completely acceptable for Mom to love again and build a new life with another man. Approached properly, children of any age can be helped to see that your marriage to a new man does not at all detract from the love that they feel for their father and given time, they will also welcome the presence of new love in their home.

## The Question-and-Answer Portion of the Program

Your children are going to have a whole bunch of questions for you, at the heart of which are going to be fears and concerns. Let's examine some of the most common questions as well as suggested responses by you:

### Q. "How could you do this to (or forget about) Daddy?"

As you have no doubt done in the past, assure your children that you are by no means "doing" anything to Daddy. You are certainly not "forgetting Daddy"; you will always love Daddy and you will always treasure the time that all of you shared. However, your response will also need to include a gentle yet firm reminder that their father is now gone and that he of all people wanted you—and his children—to be happy.

Assure your children that you will continue to celebrate Daddy's memory and remember him on birthdays, holidays and in all of the ways that you have done in the past—and then make sure that you do so!

## Q. "What do I / we call him?" (This may also take the form of, "I'm NOT calling him Daddy!")

You must defer to whatever makes your children the most comfortable—not what you and/or what your intended would prefer. They may have no problem calling him "Dad" or "Daddy-Joe" or "Uncle Joe". On the other hand, they may be comfortable continuing to call him by his first name. It may stay that way forever or it may evolve into something more personal over time.

Take also into consideration the fact that while they may want to refer to Joe as "Daddy", they might feel guilty in doing so; as if they were dishonoring the memory of their late father. Reassure them that calling your new husband "Daddy" by no means implies that they have "forgotten" their late father and that if they are comfortable in doing so, referring to your new husband as "Dad" is perfectly fine.

Whatever their choice, it remains their choice and you cannot force the issue. You need to be far more concerned with creating a new family dynamic, not what everyone's titles are going to be.

## Q. "He's not MY father!"

Not a question on its face, but naturally, with the addition of another authoritative presence, the question hiding behind this declaration is, **"Do I have to listen to him?"**

Of course, the answer is yes.

At one time or another, and under the best of circumstances, all children will try to "play" one parent against the other. When there is an addition of another "head of household" or the blending of families and/or households, there is an obvious period of adjustment—no two adults do things exactly alike, particularly when it pertains to children. This includes matters such as discipline, house rules, responsibilities and privileges.

The key here will be constant communication between you and your man, so that you can present a necessary united front to your children. For example, if one of you tends to be stricter than the other, this merits serious discussion away from the children. If your intended has no children of his own (and thus no direct parenting experience), you will need to be quite patient while he adjusts to his new and "ready-made" family. He, in turn, will need to respect your expertise and knowledge as the experienced parent, while you *patiently* explain reasons and rationale behind decisions that you make on behalf of the children. In other words, "because I said so" won't work with your man either.

Conversely, your prospective husband-to-be cannot expect to come in and change and upend all of the rules by which your children have been living; particularly older children. If your sixteen-year-old has been dating for a year, your man cannot come blazing in, insisting that they are not permitted to date until they are seventeen. If a child's curfew is 11:00 p.m., he cannot reasonably expect to change it to 9:00 p.m. If your eight–year-old listens to music before going to sleep, that has to be permitted to continue and so forth. Bear in mind that this principle also works in the other direction; if your partner has children, you cannot change or overturn their longstanding rules or parameters either.

In turn, your children should treat the new addition(s) to your exist-ing family with respect and regard. If there is a disagreement on how an issue should be handled, it needs to be discussed openly and first between the two of you. Avoid "taking sides"—on either side! Most of all—be patient! The adjustments will happen—but as with everything else, these adjustments take time as well.

## Q. "Are you going to have more children?"

Being a young widow, the chances are excellent that you may want to add to your family; especially if your new love has no children. This question calls for honesty, and I'm assuming that you have, of course, discussed whether or not you are going to have children with your prospective husband. Here again, I do not believe in "surprises".

If you are in fact planning on having another child or more children, share this to the best of your ability. While you can't exactly say, "Yes, we're having another child and it will arrive on thus-and-such day," let your children know that you and your new partner have discussed this subject and that having more children is something that you would very much like to do in the future or, at the very least, is a distinct possibility.

Most importantly, convey the reassurance that another child or more children will not interfere with or change your feelings toward them—and yes, older children need this reassurance too.

## Q. "What about 'our time'?" (referring to your "alone time" spent with just you and your children. You are especially likely to hear this if you have been widowed for a longer period of time and your children have become accustomed to having you to themselves.)

I have always fervently believed that in any successful family paradigm, there are several "lives" involved: your life individually, your husband's life individually, your life as a couple, your life as a family and each parent individually with the children. For example, while Kendall has always enjoyed her time alone with me, she will also speak glowingly and lovingly about the time that she was able to spend alone with her dad. The very special time that you spend alone with your children must continue and your new love will need to understand this.

Even though there is the addition of another head of household, you should continue to make the time for those trips to the park or the mall or overnighters out of town or cheeseburger runs with just you and your children. At the same time, you can also encourage your new love to spend time alone with your children…without forcing things; it can also be a fun and important time of bonding, where they can start their own traditions and outings.

## Q. "Where are we going to live?"

Children primarily crave two things—security and routine. Like peanut butter and jelly, movies and popcorn or shoes and…well, more shoes, one logically goes with the other. The combining of two households naturally poses the question of who moves in with whom? Again, these are things that must be discussed with your new love prior to broaching the subject with your children. Simply answering, "I don't know" or "We haven't figured that out yet" means that your children are going to go to bed worried about where they're going to be waking up. The older the children, the worse the fear will be, as older children are more firmly ensconced in their schools, with their friends and activities.

I would be quite age-sensitive in considering this issue. For example, if the child is in his or her junior or senior year of high school, I would be most reluctant to uproot the child at that point in his or her life; to the point that where the child was geographically unable to continue in the current school, I might postpone moving and/or marriage until after graduation. Marriage can wait a few months or for a year; this time in your child's life is but once. Younger children will be slightly more adaptable; although they too will have trepidation at the thought of leaving the familiar behind. It will be up to both of you to allay their fears. Don't trivialize their feelings or sweep this subject under the carpet with the proverbial, "You'll just make new friends".

Choose to discuss these subjects with your children with compassion, understanding and sensitivity, instead of a "this is what I'm doing and you have no choice in the matter" attitude. Dispel their fears of an uncertain future and couple that with the reassurance that their father will always be remembered with the utmost love and respect. This way, the prospect of remarriage and the formation of a "new" family can be an exciting prospect indeed.

## The Fine Print

I consider myself one of the most romantic people on the planet, so it pains me to have to bring up something as unromantic as finances. Once again, I state unequivocally and in my very best English...

Yuck.

Romance aside, it would be downright foolhardy to ignore what could happen to any financial benefits that you are receiving as a widow. You must consider these fiscal ramifications prior to remarriage. For example, if you and/or your children are receiving Social Security survivor benefits, you may forfeit or compromise these benefits upon remarriage. In fact, Social Security sends periodic questionnaires to regularly update information on survivor benefit recipients and whether or not you have remarried is asked on that questionnaire.

The same may hold true for any kind of survivor pensions that you are receiving as a widow from your husband's employment as well as any continued health care insurance—all of these benefits may be compromised or forfeited altogether upon remarriage. The exception to this of course is any lump sum life insurance payouts that you received immediately after the death. As the spouse of your late husband, you were likely the primary beneficiary and these previously paid claims are yours to keep.

As to all of the other benefits, there's no such thing as a "do-over". In other words, should your subsequent marriage end in divorce, you can't go back to the powers-that-be and say, "Okay, I'm a widow again; crank up the benefits." I realize that you're in love and the world is once again a beautiful place; however, as wholly unromantic as this is, we also know that at least 50 percent of the marriages in the United States end in divorce. I do know that he has assured you many times over that "we're different" and that "there's nothing to worry about" and that he's "going to take care of you", but you have the benefit of experience now; learn from that experience!

The most prudent advice here is DO YOUR HOMEWORK and do your homework thoroughly! You must rationally and objectively weigh the potential financial consequences of a remarriage versus your overall long-term financial picture—especially if there are children involved. Since every case is different, consult with your accountant, as well as directly with any and all companies and/or government entities from whom you may be receiving any kind of survivor benefits (either for yourself or on behalf of your children) to inquire what their specific policies are concerning remarriage. Do not simply make assumptions or decide, "Well, this is what happened to Susie when she went through this, so I'll be treated the same way." Or worse yet, you just ignore the whole situation in favor of a very rude surprise later on. While it's true that you are a young widow, you cannot afford to be "young and foolish" when it comes to your financial future and the financial future of your children.

Most of all, do not allow yourself to be cajoled or badgered into relinquishing benefits or acting in a rash manner regarding finances—by *anyone*. This is your future of which we are speaking. This is perhaps your lifetime security and the security and future inheritance belonging to your children. There is no room for guilt here and anyone who attempts to make you feel guilty in this respect or make you feel like you are "all about the money" —whether it's your man or your mother—needs to be schooled in the ways of common sense.

## Spell It Out

We continue with the decidedly "unromantic" portion of the program with the discussion of—gulp—the prenuptial agreement.

Without sounding terribly harsh, and because this is a subsequent marriage for at least one of you and possibly both of you, it would again be completely irresponsible to re-enter into marriage without a discussion of "who keeps what". Especially important if you live in a community property state, it is extremely wise to execute a basic prenuptial agreement that simply spells out two vital points:

- All property and assets that each of you is bringing into the marriage. This includes *all* real assets (your home, any undeveloped land, etc.), liquid assets (money and all other cash holdings) and personal assets (vehicles of all kinds, including boats, motorcycles, off-road vehicles, etc., works of art in any form, jewelry, electronics, mementos and any other valuables). This is to protect and retain personal property belonging to each of you and this property should be disclosed up-front and in full.
- Should the marriage come to an end, how all jointly acquired assets (purchases that you have made as a couple) will be divided.

We no longer live in an age where "the wife automatically 'gets' it all" in a divorce. You must each protect what is rightfully yours; especially where children are concerned. This may be a difficult or awkward discussion to have and you may be met with, "that's *so* unromantic; nothing bad is going to happen" (coincidentally, the same excuse invoked by very naive men during the discussion of condom usage.)

The document does not have to be long or fancy; it simply needs to detail what you are bringing into the marriage and how jointly acquired assets will be divided. In order to execute a valid prenuptial agreement, you may wish to consult a Lawyer Referral Service to see what the law requires in the state or country where you live.

### CAROLE'S "REALLY UNROMANTIC" REMARRIAGE REMINDERS

I agree that this part of the remarriage question is the most difficult and is also a huge lovey-dovey buzz kill. However, as a young widow you now also have the advantage of knowing about being prepared—or more importantly, what may happen if you're not prepared!

Before you head full-speed into the marriage arena once more, you must take careful stock of the following considerations. Use this checklist as your investigative tool, so that you will have all of the information that you need to make a wise and informed decision regarding remarriage.

**1. List *all* of the entities from which you receive monetary or insurance benefits on an ongoing basis. These entities may include Social Security, Veterans Administration, survivor pension issuer(s), retirement pension issuer(s), medical/dental insurance companies, etc. Include the telephone number(s) beside each:**

_____

_____

_____

_____

_____

**2. a. In contacting each one of these entities, use this "script" as a guideline:**

*"I'm calling to inquire as to whether or not a possible remarriage will affect or modify my continued receipt of benefits* for me [and/or for your children if applicable]."

**b. After you have been given an answer:**

*"Would you please send me a confirmation of that in writing for my records? Thank you so much."*

Be absolutely sure to write down exactly what you are told as well as with whom you spoke and the date on which the conversation took place and calendar to follow up on the written confirmation. A written confirmation is vital; you don't want anyone trying to rescind any assurances that were made to you regarding your continued receipt of benefits.

You must be just as prudent and thorough with this aspect of your remarriage consideration as you were when you were a new widow and first filing for benefits. Your financial future is not to be foolishly gambled with or otherwise "ignored"; even in the name of love.

Now that you have completed your financial "detective work", it is time to sit down with your love and talk about all of the factors that need to be taken into consideration prior to remarriage. Again, I realize that this is not a very romantic (or necessarily pleasant) task; however, under your rather unusual set of circumstances, it is a task that is well worth the undertaking.

Plan this discussion with your prospective husband to take place when the two of you are alone; at one of your homes and without children present. Turn off all cell phones, make a pot of coffee or tea and...

**3. a. Discuss these issues with your intended:**

- The results of your financial investigation and the impact (if any) that it might have on the question(s) of remarriage.
- The necessity for a prenuptial agreement.

**b. Any and all "practical" considerations. This may include:**

- Who is going to move in with whom?
- Will either one of you have to change jobs due to relocation? How might such a change impact your respective careers?

- Will children (belonging to either partner) have to change schools? Please also take the potential emotional and academic ramifications of such changes into careful consideration. A kindergartner who has to change schools will not endure the same emotional and/or academic consequences as a child who may be transitioning from middle school to high school or is nearing the end of his or her high school career as a junior or senior.

  c. **All of the "emotional" considerations. These may include:**

- The emotional effect that remarriage will have on your children who have already lost a father as well as your man's willingness to understand and adjust to this particular emotional vulnerability.
- The emotional effect that remarriage will have on his children; coming into a family dynamic where catastrophic loss has been experienced.
- Whether you plan to have more children and the impact that these plans may have on the children of both partners.
- Longstanding family and household "rules", responsibilities, etc., in your respective homes as well as any expectation(s) of change or modification to the same.

  Remember earlier when you learned that "grief avoided will come back to bite you"? The same rule of thought applies here. Blithely and blissfully proceeding ahead with a remarriage without addressing these very real and important issues can easily result in emotional and/or financial disaster later on. Don't foolishly avoid these subjects now in the interest of romance and take a chance on getting "bitten" later!

  Regardless of how you will ultimately answer your own question of "to remarry or not to remarry", I sincerely applaud you at having reached this moment in time. To have sufficiently healed your mind, your heart and your spirit, to have met and have a serious relationship with another person with whom you want to share love and life and to lovingly guide and include your children takes a woman of incredible fortitude, courage and love. I wish you all of the joy that you have so rightfully earned!

### Chapter 15

# WELCOME TO THE REST OF YOUR LIFE
## (And Other Parting Thoughts)

As we conclude this time spent together, it is my fervent hope that I have been both able to ease and help you along on the healing journey of young widowhood—with knowledge, insight and perhaps, even with a little bit of laughter. It is both my life's passion and my mission to contribute to the changing of and hopefully, the improvement and the enhancement of all lives that have been touched by widowhood. Through teaching, motivation, humor, education, inspiration and most of all, love; the love that we, as the incredible sisterhood known as womankind instinctively share, my goal is to reach many women just like you with a message of hope for your brighter future.

---

### FROM THE STILETTO FILE

I recall one particular conversation that I had with Mike shortly before his death. We were both acutely aware that our time together was coming to an end soon and we were discussing all of the awful-but-necessary things that one must discuss at such a critical time.

---

Along with his last wishes and what he wanted for Kendall and for me, Mike had expressed one strong desire specifically. He asked me to "take the experience and use it for good by sharing it with others."

I agreed wholeheartedly to do so, having not the foggiest idea what he meant at the time.

With time came understanding, however, and with that understanding came the certainty that others needed to be able to learn from these experiences—in the hope that those on similarly difficult or challenging journeys in life would discover that they are not alone and that life can once again be full of light and happiness.

While I know that yours has been a difficult period of adjustment, I also know that with time and patience with yourself, you have begun to grow into your new life—an unexpected life, true; a different life, definitely—but as you are also learning, it is also a life that can be just as enriching and fulfilling as the life that you are leaving behind. It would then be inaccurate to entitle this chapter, "The End", because it really is "The Beginning" for you! As you have begun moving through your healing journey, you stand on the once-shaky and now-solid foundation that was yesterday, holding the reward that is today and gazing upon the promise that tomorrow most certainly holds.

## "So What's It Like—Really?"

One question that I am commonly asked (besides "Do you _really_ wear stilettos?") is, "How is your life now..._really_?" My response, as always, is absolutely honest—I've never been very good at hiding my true feelings and I'm not about to start trying to do so now.

My life now is awesome.

Ask me if it were the life that I had envisioned for myself and like you, I would answer "of course not" in the strongest of terms.

Who on earth foresees widowhood at a young age? We have already learned that at this age, we're "supposed" to have a husband, 2.5 children, a white picket fence with a white picket fence mortgage, two cars in the driveway and assorted pets running around. Not a one of us signed up for widowhood to happen so soon.

It's a funny thing about the journeys that we are set upon by life though; sometimes those journeys can take you in completely unexpected directions. Sometimes the paths are dark and scary; full of sinkholes and fog and thunderclouds and huge detours—much like the path called young widowhood.

But as time passes and as your healing journey continues, you will turn a corner—and you're on a new path, one that's a little brighter and a whole lot smoother. This is the path that I walk now. Life really is wonderful; albeit in a different way than I could ever have expected. Though the journey wasn't always easy or pleasant, I look in the mirror now and see a woman of strength, faith and courage—the same qualities that you should be seeing in yourself right this minute.

Even if you have read this entire book and you consider yourself "back at chapter 1" on your healing journey, *you must persevere.* Read this book over and over if necessary. Find other books, audio aids and motivational materials to complement your healing journey. Visit **www.widowswearstilettos.com** and visit often; not only to be a part of the vast community of support, but also to continue your education and motivation through the resources that you will find at the site.

**The Choice is *Always* Yours!**

I have more wonderful news for you. Every single morning, when you first open your eyes...

## You Have A Choice

I realize that you don't get to choose whether or not to pay the bills or clean the house or sit in the traffic—but you *do* have a choice in how you are going to face every day—and ultimately, how you are going to face your life. You *do* have a choice in how you are going to live the rest of your life—for *you are still here,* a fact that bears repeating over and over again! You *do* have a choice with your *attitude;* the one with which you welcome the day, the one with which you interact with your children and the way you "meet, greet and treat" everyone around you.

I personally choose to smile. A lot.

Does my choice to smile mean that people don't let me down or make me angry or otherwise test my faith or hurt my heart or drop me on my head? Naturally, they do. (Figuratively speaking, of course, but it hurts just the same!)

Does the choice to smile mean that things don't get rough or that I don't have irritations or aggravations or disappointment? Of course not. There certainly are days when the cat throws up, my daughter doesn't replace the toilet paper when she's used the last of the roll, there's a major traffic jam on the freeway (usually when I'm late for something somewhere) and the mailman brings a *way*-too-high cell phone bill.

Every single day, *all* of us encounter people who might be rude or petty or insincere; others who "over-promise" and "under-deliver"; perhaps those whom we have trusted in vain and by whom we have been emotionally wounded as a result: the list goes on and on. When these things occur, I'm generally not smiling and I will admit to occasionally using very colorful and descriptive language as well.

However, I absolutely refuse to let "the small stuff" or the "small people" govern my life. Most of what we let get to us is "small stuff" or "small people". Not the young widow though! We "step over the small" and <u>move on</u>. Look at what we've been through, you and I; what is the world going to throw at us that we can't handle?

More often than not, my sentences are prefaced with, "I am so excited", because I usually am excited about something. When someone asks how I'm doing, I am genuinely excited! Be it over my beautiful daughter's latest academic feat or cheerleading competition; watching my amazingly talented "adopted daughter" perform onstage or onscreen; traveling all over and meeting new people like you; getting together with friends over cocktails or receiving the invitation announcing a sale from my favorite department store, I *am excited.*

Remember when we talked about Energy Drainers? They can't *stand* me. They make fun of me. They want to hit me over the head with a brick, because I'm so for-real excited! I'm excited about life, my family, my loved ones, my dearest friends, the people I'm going to meet and where life is going to lead me next. I am resolute in my refusal to lead a half-baked, homogenized, lukewarm, ho-hum, blasé, just-getting-by, non-passionate existence.

How about you?

You are in the middle of one of the most profound discovery processes that you will ever realize – the birth of a "you" that you may have never imagined to exist. That's a very exciting prospect...*choose* to be excited!

## JUST FOR YOU
### How Big is "Too Big?"
Throughout my many travels and in my different teaching, coaching and lecturing experiences, one of my most favorite questions that I pose to an audience is:

---

## What is it in your life that is so BIG that it has either the right or the ability to keep you from your dreams?

---

Think about it. What is it that is *so* huge in your life that it has either the ability or the power to keep you from living a life of abundance? What is it that you are allowing to stop you from having all of the happiness that you deserve?

I hope, indeed I pray, that your answer is …

---
## ABSOLUTELY NOTHING!
---

Nothing in your life should be *so* big, *so* insurmountable, *so* enormous that you allow it to stop you from getting every single thing that you deserve. Be it a position at work, financial security, a healthy mind, a healed heart, the ability to walk in four-inch heels; whatever it is that you desire most, you DO have the capacity to decide that *nothing* and *no one* is going to keep you from achieving whatever it is in life that you want to achieve.

This determination and resolve must also extend to include the circumstances surrounding your husband's death. As difficult as it may be to grasp and as selfish as it sounds, it is now *your turn*. Let me say that again.

---
## IT IS NOW YOUR TURN
---

It is now time for *you* to become all that you were meant to be, go after dreams that you have had to either postpone or perhaps abandon altogether and move into a life that you have earned and feel ready to embrace. Do not let *anything*, real or imagined, past, present or future, **including** the loss of your husband, become so big that it keeps you from having whatever it is that you seek in life or prevent you from becoming whoever and whatever it is that you want to become. You have been a wonderful wife to your late husband. Without a doubt, you have done and continue to do the best that you possibly can in raising your children. Rest well in the knowledge that you have done all of the right things for everyone.

## Ending Anger and Negative Emotions
There is no argument—you were dealt a raw deal when your husband was taken from you, irrespective of the circumstances that surrounded his

death. Even the most spiritual among us will experience more than a few moments of anger; along with a whole bunch of unanswered questions, the first of which is usually, "Why Me?" To me however, the greater pity, if not outright sin, would be to stay in that place of anger or "in the bitter" or in the fetal position or in everlasting mourning or in whatever negative emotion that might prevent you from moving forward into a life of abundance and happiness—the life that you *so* deserve; particularly after everything that you have been through and subsequently survived. We all have the *right* and are entitled to live a life of abundance and fulfillment— do not ever forget that message.

Yes, there is a mourning period, but so, too, must that mourning period come to an end. Are there times when you will miss your late husband—even after you have moved forward into a "new life"? Absolutely. However, the time to let mourning *govern* your life will come to its rightful and appropriate conclusion.

Finally, my friend, I hope you now accept a major source of comfort of which we've spoken before:

---

## YOU REALLY ARE NOT "ALL ALONE"

---

There are so many young widows out there who are struggling emotionally; too many of us in fact to have to try to "make it alone" or "put on a brave front" or feel otherwise isolated. One of my greatest goals is to continue the dialogue between every single one of us. We need to be able to talk, to cry, to laugh and to share in the common denominator that is our unique experience as young widows.

If you have questions or experiences to share or just plain old "need to get 'it' off your chest" —don't keep it "bottled up" (remember our explod- ing soda can!). Please write to me at **www.widowswearstilettos.com** and share with me, because whatever it is that you are feeling or experiencing, I understand—along with millions of other women just like you. Or visit the message boards on the website and make friends with others who relate to exactly what you're going through—because they are going through it too!

In closing, I wish you and those you love total happiness and an abundant peace as you continue forward on your new life's journey. It has been my honor to have been able to share a part of the way with you.

"The Beginning."

## WIDOWS WEAR STILETTOS "HEART MONITOR"

Let's now compare your healing journey progress from the time that you began the book to this moment. We will be able to see how far you have come and in what areas you still feel like there is progress yet to be made. Remember, there is no "right or wrong" here; nor is this a race! If you feel exactly the same as you did when you started reading the book…that's okay!

**After completing the book and having implemented either all or some of the suggestions, ideas, exercises and quizzes in it, how are you feeling right now, at this very minute?**

_____

_____

_____

_____

_____

**Without looking at your answers from chapter 1 (yet), in what areas do you feel as though you have progressed? Be sure to write down everything; no accomplishment is "too small". Whether you have improved and/or restored your health, tried a new recipe or gone out on your first date, it all counts! Write your experiences down here.**

_____

_____

_____

_____

_____

Remembering that this is not a "race" and that you have learned that your healing timeline is yours alone, in what areas do you feel as though you have not progressed either at all or as much as you would like?

_____

_____

_____

_____

_____

List three things that you either have done or that you *want* to do to help overcome whatever it is that *you* feel is preventing you from moving forward.

_____

_____

_____

_____

_____

Now, go back and compare your answers from the quiz in chapter 1 to your answers here. Are there any differences?

a. Yes

b. No

What specific differences do you see or feel? Again, list everything here—there's no such thing as a "small change" or a little bit of progress" on this journey—it's ALL a big deal!

_____

_____

_____

_____

_____

What specific things are you committed to working on in the next six months?

_____

_____

_____

_____

_____

**\*I WILL MAKE A NOTE ON MY CALENDAR TO COME BACK TO THIS PAGE SIX MONTHS FROM TODAY'S DATE.**

## SIX MONTH CHECKUP

Let's see how you're doing since you initially took this quiz at the time that you finished reading the book:

Today's date:_____

After having implemented either all or some of the suggestions, ideas, exercises and quizzes in the book, how are you feeling right now, at this very minute?

_____

_____

_____

_____

_____

Without looking at your previous answers (yet), in what areas do you feel as though you have progressed? Once again, be sure to write down everything, no matter how "small".

_____

_____

_____

In what areas do you feel as though you have not progressed either at all or as much as you would like—in other words, you still feel "stuck"?

_____

_____

_____

_____

_____

List three things that you have either done or that you *want* to do to help overcome whatever it is that *you* feel is preventing you from moving forward.

_____

_____

_____

_____

_____

Now, go back and compare your answers from six months ago to your answers here. Are there any differences?

a. Yes

b. No

What specific differences do you see or feel?

_____

_____

_____

_____

_____

_____

_____

What specific things are you committed to working on in the next six months?

_____

_____

_____

_____

_____

*I WILL MAKE A NOTE ON MY CALENDAR TO COME BACK TO THIS PAGE SIX MONTHS FROM TODAY'S DATE.

## ONE YEAR CHECKUP

Let's check in one more time and chart your progress:

Today's date:_____

After having implemented either all or some of the suggestions, ideas, exercises and quizzes in the book, how are you feeling right now, at this very minute?

_____

_____

_____

_____

_____

Without looking at your previous answers (yet), in what areas do you feel as though you have progressed? Once again, be sure to write down everything; no matter how "small".

_____

_____

_____

In what areas do you feel as though you have not progressed either at all or as much as you would like—in other words, you still feel "stuck"?

_____

_____

_____

_____

_____

List three things that you have either done or that you *want* to do to help overcome whatever it is that you feel is preventing you from moving forward.

_____

_____

_____

_____

_____

Now, go back and compare your answers from six months ago to your answers here. Are there any differences?

a. Yes

b. No

What specific differences do you see or feel?

_____

_____

_____

_____

_____

_____

_____

_____

What specific things are you committed to working on in the next six months?

_____

_____

_____

_____

_____

_____

_____

_____

_____

_____

_____

_____

_____

_____

_____

_____

_____

_____

_____

_____

_____

_____

_____

_____

_____

_____

## CAROLE'S HAPPILY-EVER-AFTER
## "CLIP AND COMMIT"
## COMMITMENT CONTRACT

### I PROMISE WITHOUT FAIL:

- To treat myself with honor and respect in all manner of life. My self-talk will be impeccable, as will the way in which I care for myself. There is no room in my life for destructive behaviors, habits or anything else meant to otherwise compromise my healing journey and as such, these things will not be a part of my life.

- To recognize that mine is a **healing** journey, that it is my journey *alone* and that I will have patience with myself and with the process. I know that I will have good days as well as challenging days; however, I will keep moving **forward**.

- To understand that the same philosophies apply to my children. To that end, I will not rush them or decide for them when their grieving should end. Should they need help coping with the loss of their father, I will seek help from appropriate experts on their behalf.

- To seek additional help for myself if I need it and I will do so when that need arises. I will further continue to avail myself of support and education in the form of books, audio aids, websites and any other support systems that will enhance my healing journey.

- To continue to journal my feelings and revisit my writings in this book in order to track my progress.

- To not put on a "front" or be otherwise dishonest about my grief; either with myself or with those around me.

- To not let the unsolicited opinions of others either hurt or deter me from the constructive life that I have chosen to lead.

- To recognize that widowhood is an experience, which while I did not seek it out, has made me a stronger, wiser and more compassionate woman. Widowhood does not define who I am; rather, it's an experience that I have survived. It is not a journey that I sought; nonetheless, it is a journey that I am learning to embrace.
- To understand that I am entitled to a life filled with happiness, abundance and peace and to actively pursue that life accordingly.

# EPILOGUE

…and as the sun set over the hillsides
and the chill of a December evening quietly fell,
while still holding tightly to her daughter's hand…
the young widow bid her beloved
a tearful "I'll love you forever" and a final farewell;
and she did so in four-inch black slingback pumps,
because, after all…
…widows wear stilettos.

# ACKNOWLEDGMENTS

The author gratefully acknowledges and definitely would have never made it this far without the following people; all of whom, without exception, have helped her to reach this moment in time.

The most unbelievable team of talent and vision that an author and writer could ever hope to have: Agents, Ink.: you are where it all "began"; what would I have done without you! My amazing and remarkable contributor; also starring in the lead roles of confidante, head cheerleader and all-around literary sage, Sydney Harriet, Ph.D., Psy.D.—I happily share this moment on the "journey" with you. My publisher, visionary and "guardian angel", Dr. Joan S. Dunphy, along with Justin Gross, JoAnne Thomas, Ron Hart and everyone at New Horizon Press, this project could not possibly have found a better "home" and I sincerely appreciate and thank all of you—it's nothing short of a joy working with all of you. My publicity and media geniuses, coaches and mentors: Dan Janal/Janal Communications; Steve Harrison, along with Bill Harrison, Ginny Shephard, Gail Snyder, Nick Summa and the entire "team" at Bradley Communications and Stacy Rollins at Warner Bros./Telepictures; our message would never have reached the media without your expertise and guidance and I am so blessed to have been student to your collective tutelage. For the "audio portion of the program", my deepest thanks to Larry Russell and WTS Media for all for your creative wisdom and support.

Karen Ronne Tupek and Penguin 51 Productions: without you, there would be no global *Widows Wear Stilettos* and your dedication (which I absolutely believe to be twenty-four hours a day) is incredible—I love you to pieces. Lastly, where would I be without the "Glam Squad": Teddie Tillet, Ashley Elkins Hoffman, Anosh-y-Hambarsom, Jonathan Alcorn and Jun Jeong/Star Image…many thanks and love to all of you for helping me be the best "me" humanly possible—even first thing in the morning! My deepest thanks go out to every single one of you for taking on this most important mission alongside me and believing in it so passionately.

Lee Woodruff, many thanks to you for your time, your advocacy, your ear and your assistance in helping us reach an audience who so badly needs to hear what we have to say—I am so grateful to you for sharing your advice, your wit and wisdom. Much gratitude and thanks also to the Woodruff family for sharing you with the entire world—you are indeed a gift.

The Santa Ana Police Department, Santa Ana, California; the Santa Ana Police Officers Association; Chief Paul Walters; Mark Nichols and Kenneth Hannegan, Esq., for your support and assistance to our entire family. Special thanks and love to: Barry Davies, Gary Nickens, Gary and Kathy Bruce, Jay and Susan Miller and Anthony Bertagna for bringing comfort and light into our home when we could not have been more in need.

The women of Mary Kay Cosmetics who have touched my life and taught me well; most especially, Rena Tarbet, Linda Toupin, Kristina Boyd, Heidi Marbach, Gay Hollar, Sandra Tatzer, Sandy Bush, Barbara de Lachica and last, but never least, my dear lifelong friend, Nanci Alderson-Cooley. It is because all of you so generously shared your talent, guidance and love that I have been able to realize dreams I might never have otherwise seen to fruition.

The congregation of Temple Beth David, Westminster, California, for supporting our family in so many ways for so very many years. A very special thanks and love to Hallie, Joel, Devin and Sydney Berman; Brooke, David, Shara and Justin Thibault; Sharon and Larry Matalon; Deanne and Richard Ruby; Penny Davis, Gloria Schwartz, Rabbi Kelly and Rob Gludt, for hot meals and "sick" visits, "kid runs", sitting for hours on end in emergency rooms and for making our days a lot brighter and the nights a lot easier—I love you so much.

The Ritz Restaurant and Garden, Newport Beach California; especially our precious Beccy Rogers, Noelle Williamson, Stacy Beech, Moises Mejia, Jeff Wermuth, Arthur Shegog and Walter "Uncle Stretch" Yong: through laughter and tears, celebrations and sorrow, you have been there for all of us. I thank all of you with love for your support and your many kindnesses to our entire family.

Rabbi Michael Mayersohn, your wisdom helped my family find peace when it didn't seem possible and helped me not only to reaffirm my own faith, but also to help me find the courage to fulfill my lifelong dream by embarking on this adventure called writing. I am forever indebted to you.

Bobby Slayton, your brilliance and humor during the darkest days of our lives and especially during Mike's last days will never truly be repaid— you were then, as you are now and will forever be "Uncle Bobby"…and our hero. Teddie Tillett Slayton, your heart, your humor and your friendship mean everything to me…you are without a doubt my "rock", my "extra right arm" and one of the most important influences in my life. For everything that both of you have done and continue to do (like helping me to find the "skull" within!), for showing me how to laugh again and most of all, for teaching me that it was okay to *start* laughing again, the words "thank you" to both of you will never really be adequate.

Natasha "Tashie" Slayton, Shannon "Shan The Man With A Plan" Crouss, Courtney Erin Williamson, Chelsey Nicole Williamson (of blessed memory), Sarah LeAnn Snyder and Cassandra Gynelle Johnson: you are my "daughters" of the heart; the precious angels for whom I didn't have to get stretch marks in order to love as my own. My pride in each of you brings tears to my eyes and your "Mommy C" loves you so very much.

Sharla Ashton Sanders, Debra Boyd, Susan Snyder-Borg and Diane Fahrenkrug: You have each believed in me unwaveringly for most of my life. Thank you for your support, your love and your "sisterhood"; it's a gift that I treasure each and every day.

No one is more fortunate than I to have the family with whom I am blessed. Many thanks and much love especially to David Clinkenbeard, Russell Gilbert, M.D., Deborah Gilbert and Linda and Max Ciampoli for your support and enthusiasm for this project from its inception. Much love and gratitude as well to every single member of the Williamson, Bobinsky and Zimmer families—I love you all desperately.

Dave Stansbury: My partner in my new life, my partner in love and "Vice President In Charge..."; you are the person who lives his life as an example for others to follow—integrity without compromise; love without condition and strong, yet always yielding. Most are people of only words; you instead are a man of action—always giving more than taking; always offering more than asking. For never permitting me to give up or give in, for your resolute belief in me, for your endless patience, for proudly standing next to me and for always standing behind me—even when I didn't realize that you were there, for your wonderful humor and love of condensed milk, "windscreen wipers", Ferraris, candlesticks and inventive commandeering of the remote control, for supporting me in my mission and being my future while helping to honor my past...and for so very much more—I thank you and I love you. You are all things good and positive in my life; you are a shining light and in my eyes and in my heart, you are the very definition of love.

Finally, to my Forever Friend…thank you for your unconditional friendship and for showing me that life could again be truly "vicious-delicious" and exactly like gasoline and a lit match.

# RECOMMENDED READING AND ADDITIONAL RESOURCES

## READING

### Chapter 1

Colgrove, Melba Ph.D. Harold H. Bloomfield, M.D. & Peter McWilliams, *How to Survive the Loss of a Love.* Simon & Schuster, 1976.

Staudacher, Carol. *A Time to Grieve: Mediations for Grieving After the Death of a Loved One.* HarperCollins Publishers, 1994.

Kushner, Harold S. *When Bad Things Happen to Good People.* Harper-Collins Publishers, 1981.

### Chapter 4

Berg, Rona. *Beauty: The New Basics.* Workman Publishing Company, Inc., 2001.

Aucoin, Kevyn. *Face Forward.* Little, Brown & Company, 2000.

### Chapter 6

Farrow, Joanna. *Four Ingredient Cookbook.* Anness Publishing, Ltd., 2003.

Fix It Fast, Pillsbury, General Mills, Inc., 2005.

## RESOURCES

- **FOR IMMEDIATE CRISIS INTERVENTION**: Call 911; the very kind dispatchers will immediately connect you with a Crisis Intervention hotline.

- **NATIONAL SUICIDE HOTLINE: (800) 784-2433** or **(800) 273-8255**. You can also visit on the Internet at **www.suicidehotlines.com**. For teens and parents of teens, you may visit **www.suicidalteens.com**.

- **ADDITIONAL CRISIS INTERVENTION/BEREAVEMENT AND COUNSELING:** You can locate many local agencies dealing in crisis intervention as well as bereavement and counseling in the first pages of your local telephone directories. Consult "Community Services" (or a similar title) under "Crisis Intervention". Also, you may contact your local hospital's information office for referrals.

- **SOCIAL SECURITY ADMINISTRATION**: You will find the toll free telephone numbers in your telephone book. Consult the front of the book under "Government Listings"; you will find Social Security under "United States Government Offices". You will also find Social Security on the Internet at **www.ssa.gov.**

- **DEPARTMENT OF VETERANS' AFFAIRS:** As with Social Security, you will find the toll free telephone number in your telephone book under "United States Government Offices". You will want the toll free number assigned to "Benefits Information and Claims". You will also find the Veterans Administration on the Internet at **www.va.gov**.

- **LAWYER REFERRAL SERVICE**: Under "Community Services" (or similar title) in the front pages of your telephone book, there will be listings for the local Legal Aid Society or Lawyer Referral Service as well as the local Bar Association referral line. These referral lines are free of charge and are designed to help you locate a lawyer near you who specializes in estate matters.

- **FOR MATTERS CONCERNING FILING OF FORMS WITH THE COURT**: Consult the front pages of your telephone book under "County Government". You may also locate a court's official website by typing in "[YOUR COUNTY NAME] Court official website" under any Internet search engine. The home page of your county's court will direct you as to which forms to file, how to file forms properly and the appropriate jurisdiction in which to file.

# <u>Notes</u>

# <u>Notes</u>

# <u>Notes</u>

# <u>Notes</u>

# <u>Notes</u>

# <u>Notes</u>

# Notes

# Notes

# Notes